Ottilie Mulzet has translated over 18 volumes of Hungarian poetry and prose from contemporary authors such as László Krasznahorkai, Szilárd Borbély, Gábor Schein, György Dragomán, László Földényi, István Vörös, Edina Szvoren, Krisztina Tóth and others. Her translation of László Krasznahorkai's *Baron Wenckheim's Homecoming* (New Directions, 2019) was awarded the National Book Award in Translated Literature in 2019, and her translation of Krasznahorkai's *Herscht 07769* was shortlisted for the Gregg Barrios Book in Translation Prize.

THE HUNGARIAN LIST

Under a Pannonian Sky

Ten Women Poets from Hungary

Translated by Anna Bentley, Erika Mihálycsa, Ottilie Mulzet, Ivan Sanders, Clare Pollard with Anna T. Szabó and George Szirtes

Edited with an Introduction by Ottilie Mulzet

LONDON NEW YORK CALCUTTA

The Hungarian List
SERIES EDITOR
Ottilie Mulzet

Ottilie Mulzet would like to thank the Hungarian Translators' House in Balatonfüred, Hungary, where several sections of this anthology were completed

Seagull Books, 2025

This compilation first published by Seagull Books in 2025

ISBN 978 1 8030 9 567 7

British Library Cataloguing-in-Publication Data

A catalogue record for this book is available from the British Library.

Typeset by Seagull Books, Calcutta, India

This anthology is dedicated to the memory of
Dr Evžen (Jenci) Gál

CONTENTS

Under a Pannonian Sky

INTRODUCTION

As the objects are enclosed within themselves
I stand beyond solitude, by the boundary-stone
of existence.

—Zsuzsa Beney

The inspiration for this anthology first arose in Room No. 2 in the Hungarian Translators' House in Balatonfüred, when, some years ago, I came across an anthology of Hungarian women's poetry.[1] Published in 1997, and featuring well over 100 poets writing from the sixteenth century up till the end of the second millennium, the *Anthology of Hungarian Women Poets* seemed to promise a first hopeful step in increasing the visibility of women's voices in Hungarian letters. Yet it remains a single—and isolated—document.

The present anthology is much less ambitious in scope, presenting a select group of ten women active during the second half of the twentieth century and into the new millennium. Like any anthology, its ori-

1 Margit S. Sárdi and László Tóth (eds), *Magyar költőnők antológiája* [Anthology of Hungarian Women Poets] (Budapest: Enciklopédia Kiadó, 1997).

gins are highly subjective, even if certain continuities of style or theme become evident, yet its main impulse remains simple: to present to the Anglophone reader the voices of Hungarian women, often writing in difficult times and all under the shadow of tumultuous, indeed often brutally destructive, historical events.

Anna Menyhért, the Hungarian critic who has written about early and mid-twentieth century Hungarian women authors,[2] draws attention to the absence of women in the literature textbooks of her school years, a situation that unfortunately remains largely unchanged at the time of writing.[3] This visible absence, she notes, conveys to 'the large majority of the country's population that women don't write. This, however, is not true.'[4] She characterizes the tradition of modern Hungarian women's writing as 'both hidden and [hiding] itself away in the manner of a sinking stream which comes to the surface only to vanish underground again', the result not merely of the inevitable factors of sexism or personal attitudes, but no less of the complex dynamics of Hungary's shifting processes of critical canonization and readerly reception.[5]

Rectifying the injustice of this vast gap in domestic awareness and the international translation market, or in another sense attempting to bring this 'sinking stream' to more awareness in the English-language sphere is, in short, an aim I have cherished ever since that moment in Balatonfüred years ago. At the same time, this anthology makes no claims to completeness, instead looking towards a specific section of women's literary production and experience. With birth dates spanning

2 Anna Menyhért, *Women's Literary Tradition and Twentieth-Century Hungarian Writers: Renée Erdős, Ágnes Nemes Nagy, Minka Czóbel, Ilona Harmos Kosztolányi, Anna Lesznai* (Anna Bentley trans.) (Leiden: Brill, 2020).

3 A perusal of the centralized Hungarian literature curriculum from grades 5 up to 12 reveal very few women writers. See: https://www.oktatas.hu/kozneveles/kerettantervek/2020_nat/kerettanterv_alt_isk_5_8; and https://www.oktatas.hu/kozneveles/kerettantervek/2020_nat/kerettanterv_gimn_9_12_evf. (accessed 21 May 2025).

4 Menyhért, *Women's Literary Tradition*, p. 4.

5 Ibid, p. 9.

a precise half-century between 1922 and 1972, these poets share—whether through immediate witnessing or the powerful weight of cultural memory—a common experience of tragedies and ambiguous hopes, from the horrors of Hungary's alliance in the Second World War with Nazi Germany and complicity in the murder of much of its own Jewish population through the harsh years of Stalinist rule, the brief promise of reform in 1956 and its crushing by Soviet military invasion, the cautious liberalization of the final years of Communist rule, the highly ambiguous transformations of the 1990s, and most recently the rise of a self-proclaimed 'illiberal democracy' since 2010.

Arguably, all the authors included in *Under a Pannonian Sky* could be somehow classified as 'poets of witness'—yet to leave them consigned to this designation is a strong, in many ways unjust, oversimplification. For it is not only the weight of the experience they bear, but even more compellingly the artistic strategies that they use, develop and refine to transform the realities of their lifetimes into the works of art presented here. In one sense, they all maintain, if often in quite different reactions and responses, the influence of the generation of poets known as *Újhold*, or New Moon, a cohort that emerged in the wreckage—just as much moral as it was physical—of post-Second-World-War Hungary. Associated with the literary journal bearing this title, the *Újhold* includes an impressive number of the authors who emerged as the leading creative personalities of the age, among them János Pilinszky, Iván Mándy, Miklós Mészöly, Géza Ottlik, Zoltán Jékely, György Rába, Magda Szabó, Mátyás Domokos, Sándor Weöres and, of course, Ágnes Nemes Nagy, whose work opens this anthology.

Although the journal itself only appeared from 1946 to 1948, its influence was genuinely seismic. Yet as the Communist Party tightened its grip, almost immediately after the end of the war, *Újhold* came under harsh critique—not least from György Lukács, who termed the journal 'the ivory tower protests of an isolated individual self'.[6] After further

6 Gábor Schein, *Poétikai kísérlet az Újhold költészetében* [Poetic Experiment-ation in the New Moon Group] (Budapest: Universitas Könyvkiadó, 1998), p. 17.

condemnation at the First Writers' Congress of 1949, the doors to publication were slammed shut in the face of its authors, who often returned to print only during the cultural relaxation of the 1960s.[7] Through the 1970s and 1980s, Hungary—in contrast to several of its neighbours—refrained from the worst excesses in the policing of its creative spheres: none of the authors included in this volume, for instance, was forced to publish exclusively in samizdat, or to make damaging compromises with censorship. Yet even with long records of official publication before 1989, they cannot, by any stretch of the imagination, be viewed as compliant or conformist. Rather, the resolute moral force, the inner strength of witness embodied in the spirit of the *Újhold* generation, whether as experience or legacy, preserved their independence throughout the often-troubling ambiguities of Communism's last decades, and it is a tribute to the strength and continuity of Hungarian literary culture that women writing today are still influenced by this seminal cohort of poets.

Since the lives and the works of these poets became, in the circumstances of their creative years, so intimately entwined, it only appears natural to discuss each of them individually.

Ágnes Nemes Nagy, perhaps the most 'canonized' poet in this volume, was born in Budapest in 1922. She received her diploma from the Pázmány Péter Catholic University in Hungarian, Latin and art history in 1944. Her first volume, *Kettős világban* [*In a Double World*], was published in 1946, the same year that she cofounded, with her husband, Balázs Lengyel and others (including János Pilinszky and Iván Mandy), the literary journal known as *Újhold* (New Moon, see above). *Újhold*, although published only 1946–1948, was to prove highly influential in post-war literary life. In many ways, the story of Nemes Nagy's poetry is inseparable from the story of *Újhold*, the mission of which was to confront the existential situation after the devastation of the Second World War in Hungary (as well as its wartime alliance with the Axis powers). As Nemes Nagy commented:

7 Ibid.

> All of us, including myself, who had started by writing poetry following the poetic tradition of the 1930s and the poetic heritage of the different generations of Nyugat needed to let go of this, to surpass it to a degree. To write about the extreme: about the assault on existence in a spiritual and physical sense. About physical misery and madness. We let these experiences crawl into our poems.[8]

Elsewhere, Nemes Nagy defined war as 'the most fundamental experience of my generation'.[9] With the advent of communism in Hungary almost immediately after the end of the war, *Újhold* came under harsh critique, as mentioned above. After the condemnation at the First Writers' Congress of 1949, the doors to publication were closed for Nemes Nagy and her colleagues; for at least ten years, she mainly lived from her translations of French and German literature. Nemes Nagy began to work as an independent writer from 1958 onward. Although a figure of major consequence in Hungarian letters in the late twentieth century (as for the generation following the demise of communism), she remained distant from cultural politics, although publishing at least seven volumes of poetry during her lifetime, many children's books and several essay collections, for which she is also renowned. To a degree, the isolation that was imposed upon her in the 1950s lasted until the end of her life.[10]

The poet George Szirtes—Nemes Nagy's main translator—has commented on her work: 'I have no doubt that Ágnes Nemes Nagy was one of the most important Hungarian poets of the postwar period. In fact I've no serious doubt that she is far more than this: that she is one of the great indispensable European poets of the twentieth century. This is a feeling I have had since first reading her in the 1980s. There was

8 Ágnes Lehóczky, *Poetry, the Geometry of the Living Substance: Four Essays on Ágnes Nemes Nagy*. PhD dissertation, School of Literature and Creative Writing, University of East Anglia, 2011, p. 20.

9 Ágnes Nemes Nagy, *Az elők mértana. Prózai írások* [The Geometry of the Living: Prose Writings], VOL. 1 (Budapest: Osiris Kiadó, 2004) p. 53.

10 Lehóczky, *Poetry*, p. 13.

something crystalline and vast about her work, which imposed itself on me with all the authority of mountainhood.'[11] Poet and translator Ágnes Lehóczky speaks of the 'embodied abstractions' in Nemes Nagy's work.[12]

This crystalline quality—with its suggestion of geometry, definite lines and clarity—is certainly a key descriptor of Nemes Nagy's work, which, in terms of Hungarian criticism, has often been described with the moniker 'objective lyricism.'[13] At the same time, her work is permeated with a sense of ethics: not in any kind of dogmatic sense, but stemming from the severe existential crisis that followed the destruction and genocide(s) of the Second World War. This is one of the most important legacies of the *Újhold* poets, extending to many contemporary writers even beyond the covers of this anthology, including such poets as Szilárd Borbély and Gábor Schein. Nemes Nagy's first volume *Kettős világban* [*In a Double World*] expresses this dilemma in a Cartesian sense.[14] As Schein puts it in his study of Nemes Nagy's poetics, 'After the Second World it became inconceivable to continue the poetic model of the 1930s without breakage, as well as the flattening of legitimate experience that was occurring under communist totality.'[15]

George Szirtes describes the betrayal of those years: 'Betrayal was everywhere. Betrayal stiffened [Nemes Nagy's] resolve and gave her energy. It was partly betrayal that grew into the great crystalline mountain . . .'[16] Worth mentioning as well is that Nemes Nagy and her husband at the time, Balázs Lengyel, were active in the Hungarian Resistance movement: as Lehóczky notes: 'Nemes Nagy took part in the resistance, and in her kitchen laboratory, she collaborated with friends to fabricate passports and new birth certificates for Jewish-born writers and friends.'[17]

---

11 George Szirtes, Introduction to Ágnes Nemes Nagy, *The Night of Akhenaton: Selected Poems* (George Szirtes trans.) (Highgreen: Bloodaxe Books, 2004), p. 7.

12 Lehóczky, *Poetry*, p. 10.

13 Schein, *Poétikai kísérlet*, p. 20.

14 Ibid., p. 32.

15 Ibid., p. 33.

16 Szirtes, Introduction, p. 10.

In her essay, 'Objects', Nemes Nagy wrote: 'If someone picks up, from the entirety of the world, a pebble, a leaf, a thrown-away cork stopper, some important or unimportant detail of their surroundings, it can happen that this something will become a microtransmitter in their hands, transmitting an unexpected program. It transmits the world which we know, and it also transmits what we don't know, what lies beyond recognition . . . Towards me, it is mainly objects that transmit this unknown, and so I in turn try to transmit these objects to my readers.'[18]

Nemes Nagy, despite the lack of commensurate recognition in her lifetime, remains a monumental figure in post-war Hungarian poetry, her influence on the following generations so profound as to be nearly indelible.[19]

Zsuzsa Beney, born in Budapest in 1930, first attended medical school; she graduated in 1954 and worked as a physician until the age of 70. In 1969, her work was introduced to the Hungarian reading public in an anthology, and praised by no less a poet than Sándor Weöres. Weöres's work, although very different, remained an important influence on her own, as did that of Attila József and János Pilinszky. Beney's first volume of poetry, *Tűzföld* [*Fireland*], was published in 1972, three years after her inclusion in that first anthology. She went on to publish nine volumes of poetry, several novels and four volumes of essays. Her collected works appeared in several volumes posthumously.[20] From 1992, Beney taught at the University of Pécs, and from 2000, also lectured at Miskolc University. She received her PhD in literary studies in 1993 and

---

17 Lehóczky, *Poetry*, p. 19. Lehóczky notes that Nemes Nagy and Balázs Lengyel were given the Yad Vashem Award by Israel posthumously in 1997.

18 Nemes Nagy, *Az elők mértana*, p. 33.

19 She has also proven to be influential for poets writing in English, such as Ágnes Lehóczky. See Ágnes Lehóczky, 'Nemes Nagy and Labouring in the Existence Trade', interview with Veronika Schandl, *Hungarian Literature Online*, 31 March 2020: https://hlo.hu/interview/agnes-lehoczky-nemes-nagy-and-labouring-in-the-existence-trade.html (accessed 21 May 2025).

20 Zsuzsa Beney, *Összegyűjtött versek I–III* [Collected Poems, VOLS 1–3] (Anikó Daróczi ed.) (Budapest: Gondolat Kiadó, 2008).

was made associate professor (docent) in 1998. Beney was the recipient of many prizes, including the Radnóti Prize in 2004.

As is the case with so many of the poets in this anthology, Beney's work is inextricably tied to her own life, particularly the traumatic loss of her son and husband when she was still in her thirties. Beney does not explore this double tragedy through the lens of individual narrative, but rather through allegory, particularly in her cycle of poems dedicated to the myth of Orpheus and Eurydice. As the poet and literary critic Csaba Báthori has noted, Beney returned to the myth of Orpheus and Eurydice repeatedly during her lifetime, as if to one of her own foundational myths.[21] Indeed, much of her work takes place in between the undefined and undefinable metaphysical borderlands between life and death: in her poetry, 'we are in that periphery where life and death meet; we must descend into the underworld in order to redeem a dead person to life; where life continues in death, the dead companion glances back into life . . .'[22] Her work expresses ambivalence, metaphysical doubt, hesitating between these different realms.

Beney's language is spare, she refuses ornamentation, her metaphysics are disembodied. As Weöres wrote, introducing her in 1969: '[Beney's] poems are so ethereal, that at first they hardly seem to recognize their themes, it is only after several readings that they begin to emerge. They seem immaterial, a transparent veil, and yet the material

---

21 Báthori points out as well the many resemblances between the myth of Orpheus and that of Jesus; in not a few of Beney's poems, the sense of abandonment by God is given stark expression. See Csaba Báthori, 'Volt, nincs, van–Beney Zsuzsa: *Összegyűtött versek I–III* [There Was, There Isn't, There Is: Zsuzsa Beney, *Collected Poems*, VOLS 1–3], *Magyar Narancs*, 4 September 2008: https://magyarnarancs.hu/zene2/konyv_-_volt_nincs_van_-_beney_zsuzsa_osszegyujtott_versek_i-iii-69400 (accessed 25 May 2025).

22 Csaba Báthori, 'Már csönd se vagy–Beney Zsuzsa (*1930–2006*)' [Now, You Are Not Even Silence–Zsuzsa Beney (1930–2006)], *Magyar Narancs*, 20 July 2006: https://magyarnarancs.hu/konyv/mar_csond_se_vagy_-_beney_zsuzsa_1930-2006-65794 (accessed 25 May 2025).

that resides within them has been processed in a severe manner.'[23] Of course, it is easy to see the influence of Nemes Nagy in the work of Beney, although her metaphysical inquiries carry her in a different direction; the influence of Beney's work on poets of the post-1989 generation, such as Szilárd Borbély, also seems clear, particularly in the profound movement towards immateriality and abstraction, the working of personal material into allegory and the incessant questioning of language and material form.

Ágnes Gergely was born in 1933 in Endrőd, where she spent her early childhood. Her family moved to Budapest in 1940, although summers were still spent in the country. In 1944, her father was deported for forced labour, and never returned (there are unconfirmed reports that he perished at Mauthausen). Gergely attained a degree as a teacher of Hungarian and English in 1957 at Eötvös Loránd University despite the difficulties presented by her family's 'bourgeois' background. In 1952, Gergely had also obtained a vocational certificate as an iron and metal lathe worker after being refused entrance to the University of Theatre and Film Arts for the same political reasons. After attaining her ELTE degree, Gergely taught primary and secondary school until 1963, when she chose to begin working as a journalist for Hungarian Radio. Her first volume, *You Are a Sign on My Door Post* [*Ajtófélfámon jel vagy*], was published in 1963. In 1973–1974, she was a participant in the International Writing Program at the University of Iowa. Gergely has devoted herself full time to her writing since 1988. She has published 18 volumes of poetry, 12 volumes of memoirs and prose, been awarded over 20 literary prizes, including the prestigious Kossuth Prize. She is also a distinguished and prolific translator from English; her first translations were from the work of James Joyce and Dylan Thomas, published in 1958.

23 Quoted in János Szegő, 'Áttetsző sűrűség' [Transparent Density], *Revizor Online*, 5 May 2008: https://revizoronline.com/beney-zsuzsa-osszegyujtott-versek-i-iii-hullo-ido-csond-es-hallgatas-kozott-eletem-elete/ (accessed 25 May 2025).

Gergely's extraordinary longevity means that, as a writer and poet, she has witnessed an astonishing number of different regimes, including fascism, the early communism of Stalinist Mátyás Rákosi, the late communism of János Kádár, the 'regime change' of 1989, the euphoric early 1990s and the chaos of unfettered privatization, the self-proclaimed 'illiberal democracy' instigated in 2010, and continuing to this day. Nonetheless, her work has always remained ethically and artistically independent from current prevailing political trends. Poet and critic Csaba Báthori has characterized her work as

> the protection of the memories of the memoryless, the preservation of the signs of the dead, an illuminating witness of fidelity. The poetry of Ágnes Gergely employs nearly theological weapons to hollow out its deepest channels. We observe her most characteristic words, word-families: doorpost, redemption, preservation, water-ocean, elimination, stone, cemetery-ruin-dust, Old Testament figures, and many times over: *sign*. The sign which refers to something else, to enigmatic and essential presence, which, completing this life, also directs it, diverts it, verifies it, changes it, vindicates it, renders it meaningful and lifts it up . . . Our impression here is of a long dialogue taking place with those who are distant, a dialogue which determines other aspects of human existence as well . . . [Gergely's poetry] wishes to reveal something from the world, perchance to exhume something from history, something that, without the help of poetry, would be impossible for us to see.[24]

Gergely has spoken of the extreme difficulty of coming to terms with the deportation and death of her father: 'I don't know when he died and how, which is horrific,' she related in one interview: 'That is a truly horrific feeling: person goes into the void, and there is nothing left of him.'[25]

---

24 Csaba Báthori, 'A tisztaság íze' [The Taste of Integrity], *Élet és irodalom* 49, no. 26 (July 2005).

25 Ágnes Gergely, 'I Know I Have a Guardian Angel, Sometimes It Appears in My Dreams,' interview with Gabriella Nagy, *Hungarian Literature Online*, 16

And yet she states, 'I was shocked by these things, but there is no hatred within me.'[26] Apart from the poems that address her father personally, such as 'You Are a Sign on My Door Post', Gergely has worked with allegory and symbols—particularly drawing upon her early life experience in the countryside—to convey these realities, interrogating her role in Hungarian society as a woman and as someone of Jewish heritage. In particular, she noted, in her 1978 verse novel *Kobaltország* (*Cobalt Country*):

> I had no masters. There was no one at whose feet I could have sat . . . Instead, I gained a few glimpses from the classic works of literature that were available to me, truly just a few glimpses. It is precisely because of this apparent fragility that I preserve this long-ago time, just as my favourite gemstone is the pearl, as its form is alarmingly delicate, yet it cannot be polished into pleasingly fitting metal sheets, it does not give up, and it remembers what it was born from.[27]

Gizella Hervay—one of three poets from Romania in this volume—was born in 1934 in Makó, one of many siblings. Her family was impoverished and her childhood extremely difficult.[28] In a posthumously published 'self-interview', Hervay discussed her early years, including her father's drinking, his being fired from his job during the Second World War due to having Jewish friends and the experience of standing paralysed in the street in Budapest on her way to kindergarten as German tanks rolled in one after the other like 'copulating beetles.' Hervay was in Budapest as well during the siege of 1944–1945. At her

---

March 2022: https://hlo.hu/interview/agnes-gergely-i-know-i-have-a-guardian-angel-sometimes-it-appears-in-my-dreams.html (accessed 4 December 2025).

26 Ibid.

27 Ágnes Gergely, 'Egy jazz-koncert után' [After a Jazz Concert], in *Kobaltország. Költemények versben és prózában* [Cobaltland: Poems in Verse and in Prose] (Budapest: Szépirodalmi Könyvkiadó, 1978), p.36.

28 See Gizella Hervay, *DOKUMENTUM. Hazulról haza* [Document: From Home to Home], *Lató* 2, no. 5 (May 1991): https://lato.adatbank.ro/?cid=987 (accessed 4 December 2025).

mother's initiative, she returned to Romania in 1946. Hervay received her degree in Hungarian literature and language in 1956 from Bolyai University in Cluj-Napoca, where she met her husband, Domokos Szilágyi, an important poetic influence in her life (as she was in his). She was the editor of several publications, and taught at the Hungarian Lycée of Bucharest. Her poetry began to be recognized in the early 1970s, although difficult years were to follow with the separation from her husband, and his eventual suicide in 1976. In that same year, she moved to Hungary, planning for her 15-year-old son, Attila (Kobak), to follow shortly, when he tragically perished in the Bucharest earthquake of March 1977. (The poem 'The petrified mother' [*A megkövült anya*, on p. 107] is taken from the collection that Hervay wrote after these tragedies.) Hervay, understandably, struggled tremendously in the aftermath of these losses. Her work was met with some favourable critical reception, but she had the ongoing sense that her poetry was not truly understood in Hungary, and, in the words of someone who knew her there, she felt lost in Pest.[29] In 1982, she made the decision to end her own life. Hervay wrote more than eleven volumes, including seven books of poetry and tales for children (the latter composed with her son). Hervay was awarded the Romanian Writers' Union prize in 1973, and, posthumously, the Prize for Hungarian Art in 1993.

As with the other poets in this anthology, the question of canonization arises. While Hervay's work is included in the Hungarian Digital Literary Academy,[30] in a 2010 discussion involving three women writers

---

29 Noémi Kiss, Anna Menyhért, Gabriella Nagy, and Imre József Balázs, 'Hervay Gizella–Koltő vagy költőnő?' [Gizella Hervay–Poet or Poetess?], *Korunk*, no. 4 (2022): 59–69.

30 Founded in 1998, the Digital Literature Academy [Digitális irodalmi akadémia], curated and managed by the Petőfi Literature Museum in Budapest, is meant to digitally archive and preserve the complete (in most cases) works of the most important authors of contemporary Hungarian literature, along with bibliographies, biographies, and specialist literature bibliographies. As such, it forms an important path (if certainly not the only one) to official canonization for contemporary writers. Of the writers in this volume, apart from Gizella

and a male critic who has written about Hervay, more than one participant noted that she was the only poet classed among the Romanian–Hungarian poets of her generation, while the question of her being forced into 'a normative womanly role' also arose.[31] The writer Noémi Kiss perceived traces of the influence of Paul Celan (from Bukovina), particularly in Hervay's earlier work, but again, in early criticism, Hervay was criticized for writing 'such intellectual poems' with these 'extreme visual connections'—instead, she should write about sewing needles or other womanly matters, as one reviewer opined. Yet in the view of another cited critic, Hervay developed into a good writer only once she had thrown off the mantle of Art Nouveau language, her earlier tendencies to ballad or 'folk' expression, thus becoming a true 'poet' as opposed to a mere 'poetess.'[32]

To speak of more recent critical reception, the Romanian poet and critic Imre József Balázs rightly comments on the extreme terseness of Hervay's poetry, the lack of simile, the crowded imagery of her work, which speaks of the outer world 'which cannot be spoken of', an outer world which has been emptied. There is paradoxically a distance in this work along with the release of emotion, 'a grotesque mode of seeing, given to those who perceive the omniscience of suffering.'[33] In 1984, István Ágh said of her work: 'Hervay's poetry is like fusillade from a machine gun, every bullet, every round is fatal, wounding; we are happy that we remained alive.'[34] Balázs speaks of a prophetic poetry, of 'the future made

---

Hervay, the other poets who are members of the Digital Academy are: Ágnes Nemes Nagy, Zsuzsa Beney, Ágnes Gergely, Zsuzsa Takács, Zsófia Balla, Zsuzsa Rakovszky, and Krisztina Tóth. Of the current 179 members of the Digital Academy, 15 members are women—less than 10 per cent. See: https://dia.hu/ (accessed 8 May 2025).

31 Kiss et al., 'Hervay Gizella–Koltő vagy költőnő?'

32 Ibid.

33 Imre József Balázs, 'Ki emlékszik a holnapi napra?', in *Hervay Gizella: Az idő körei. Összegyűjtött versek*, Digitális Irodalmi Akadémia, Petőfi Irodalmi Múzeum, Budapest, 2022: https://reader.dia.hu/document/Hervay_Gizella-Az_ido_korei-39910 (accessed 8 May 2025).

visible'. As part of her posthumous 'self-interview', Hervay commented: 'I reconstruct the strips of cassette tape in my head, the cries of pain that perished there. Every day a sentence comes into my mind. I note it down. There are days when the entire fates of people come into my mind.'[35]

Magda Székely was born in Budapest to an assimilated Jewish family. She was eight years old when she witnessed her mother being dragged away by a gendarme and a member of the Arrow Cross, the Hungarian fascist movement of the Second World War.[36] Székely was moved to a Catholic monastery—the nuns were openly anti-Semitic, but sheltered her, saving her life—and then placed with Swabian peasants until the end of the war.

The Hungarian writer and critic András Pályi has noted how deeply silence is rooted in Székely's poetry: it is 'the steadiest of the building blocks of her life's poetic work, its cohering strength.'[37] Clearly, this silence has to do with the unspeakable traumas of her childhood. As Székely herself relates:

> My mother was taken away on November 14 in a raid, into the death march that went along Bécsi Street. She wrote two postcards that said: Help me! Someone . . . saw her at the border. I don't know what happened to her after that. If not on the way, then she might have died in an Austrian concentration camp, maybe in Bergen-Belsen. If she even got that far . . . [My cousin and I] were handed over to some lady, then taken to Eskü Square . . . there was a mission of the Swedish Red Cross . . . they were hiding children in various church institutions they had connections with . . . [38]

Székely learnt to recite Christian prayers to conceal her identity.

---

34 Ibid.

35 Hervay, *DOKUMENTUM*.

36 Magda Székely, *Éden* [Eden] (Budapest: Belvárosi könyvkiadó, 1994), pp. xxxvii–xxxviii.

37 András Pályi, 'Székely Magda csöndjei' [The Silences of Magda Székely], *Kalligram*, no. 7 (January–February 1998).

38 Quoted in ibid.

Székely attained her degree in Hungarian and Bulgarian in 1959 at Eötvös Loránd University. From 1969–1991, she worked as an editor at the publisher Európa Könyvkiadó, and from 1991 onward, at Belvárosi Könyvkiadó. She published her first volume of poems *Kőtabla* [*Stone Tablet*] in 1962. Her second volume *Átváltozás* [*Transformation*] appeared in 1975. Altogether she was the author of nine volumes of poetry and the recipient of numerous prizes, including the Kossuth Prize in 2005. She also translated from English, Czech, Bulgarian and French. She spent the last part of her life, devoted to her writing, in relative seclusion.

There are several words for silence in Hungarian that Pályi cites, some of them indicating the absence of enunciation or falling silent (*elhallgatás, elnémulás*), as opposed to silence itself (*csönd*)—the outcome or effect of not speaking. Pályi notes that 'silence in and of itself is not poetry. But non-speaking, falling silent, is.'[39] In other words, it is a deliberate stratagem of a partial refusal of language, paring it down to its bare essentials, embracing at times as well a refusal of imagery and referentiality.

Even a cursory glance at Székely's poetry quickly reveals the extreme economy of her language, the terseness of her lines, the grammatical and semantic lacunae that might put one in mind of Emily Dickinson, although Székely often works with more 'classical' rhyming forms. To my mind, the extreme compactness of Székely's expression, her methodology of silence, would seem to have exerted an important influence on one of her successors, Szilárd Borbély, particularly in his shorter, more formal verses. Like Borbély, Székely lived an extremely quiet life: 'She was among us for decades, as if she weren't even living here.'[40]

Nemes Nagy discussed the silence in Székely's poetry in an essay devoted to her work,[41] citing, among others, the poem 'Transformation':

39 Ibid.

40 Csaba Báthori, *Néma messianizmus. Székely Magda: Albigens* [Mute Messianism: Magda Székely, *Albigens*], *Múlt és jövő* no. 3 (2014): 63–71.

41 Ágnes Nemes Nagy, 'Jegyzetek a rejtőzésről. Székely Magda versei' [Notes on Concealment: The Poems of Magda Székely], in *Az elők mértana*, pp. 433–38.

Always dispersing, then reassembling
across motion it goes
always directed towards rejuvenation
while its own self it shows.[42]

Nemes Nagy mentions that the key expression in this poem is 'directed towards rejuvenation':

> We do not know the subject [of the poem], who or what it is that disperses and reassembles a person, but . . . we cannot doubt its existential significance. It could be existence, it could be the superego, perhaps love, in any event, it is in charge of us. It hides in front of us, it shows itself and yet does not show itself, as if in gusts of wind. And if already we pronounce the word 'wind', then we are pronouncing that hidden, obscured (one of the words dearest to Székely) picture which is behind the poem, that indirect vision shrouded by abstract words. Magda Székely pulls the image into the background—in this case, to translate it roughly, the wind and a tree, or the sight of wind and sand dunes—so that the abstract (*Abstraktum*) will prevail.[43]

Nemes Nagy also notes that 'to remain authentic within the abstract image is unusual' for Hungarian poetry.[44] Not only the subject, but the object (although implicitly 'us, myself, people') is suppressed in this poem. Put more precisely, the undefined subject is granted almost omniscient presence, while the object—including the speaker of the poem—is effaced grammatically and symbolically.

I read Székely's 'A Drawing' (p. 157) as an *ars poetica*: 'Only a few / darkened lines: / hardly leaving behind / something of itself', she writes. The surface of the paper which is not drawn upon, which is left blank, is 'emancipated'. On one profound level, the stark silences and abstraction of Székely's poetry testify to the moral stance of the survivor who enacts

42 Quoted in Nemes Nagy, 'Jegyzetek a rejtőzésről', p. 437.

43 Ibid.

44 Ibid.

the paradoxical impossibility of representation in the aftermath of genocide on an unthinkable scale and horrifying mental abyss of never knowing the fate of one's loved ones.

Like Zsuzsa Beney, Ágnes Gergely, Gizella Hervay and Magda Székely, Zsuzsa Takács, born in Budapest in 1938, belongs to the generation of poets who were children at the beginning of the Second World War, meaning that the onset of Stalinist communism occurred before they reached adulthood. After completing gymnasium (academic high school), Takács applied to medical school, but was refused for political reasons: the ostensible reason was lack of space, but the real reason was the intellectual (non-proletarian) background of her family.[45] She attended classes in dramaturgy and at the Faculty of Arts at Eötvös Loránd University, where she was allowed to enrol in 1958 in the Italian, Spanish and Hungarian departments, and where she obtained a teaching certificate in Spanish and Italian. She also attended translation seminars, translating from the Latin.

Similarly to Ágnes Gergely, Takács's career as a poet has known extraordinary longevity: she first began publishing her work in literary magazines in 1964. Subsequent to this, her work was published in a 1969 anthology, and praised by János Pilinszky. Thanks to Pilinszky's praise, she was able to publish her first volume *Némajáték* [*Pantomime*] in 1970. From 1964–2001, Takács taught diplomatic history and social studies, and Spanish at the Budapest University of Economics. Takács's sojourns abroad included a year in Cuba while teaching Hungarian in 1963 and a three-month stay at the Iowa International Writing Programme in 1988. While carrying a full teaching load (until retirement in 2001) and raising a family, Takács published, between 1970 and 2021, 20 volumes of poetry, while also translating poetry from Italian, Spanish, Catalan, French and English. Takács is the recipient of numerous distinguished prizes, including the Tibor Déry Prize in 1989 and the

45 Csilla Szalagyi, *Takács Zsuzsa költészete* [The Poetry of Zsuzsa Takács] (Budapest: L'Harmattan Kiadó, 2022), p. 227.

Kossuth Prize in 2007.[46] More than one critic has referred to Zsuzsa Takács as a 'living classic'.[47]

While it is clearly difficult, if not impossible, to briefly summarize the trajectory of a poet across such a long and distinguished career, a few developments and themes can be sketched out. The recent monograph by Csilla Szalagyi[48] (also the editor of Takács's 2018 volume *Blind Hope*) surveys the poet's entire trajectory with a precise analytical lens. (It is also worth noting that, while the work of most of the poets in this volume has been discussed at length in a number of eminent literary journals, to my knowledge, Takács, Gergely and Nemes Nagy appear to be the only poets to whom complete scholarly monographs—another important aspect of both reception and canonization—have been devoted.[49] Hopefully, this situation will be remedied in the future.)

The Takács poems in this anthology largely hail from the post-1989 years up until 2018. As such, it forms part of the later development of the poet's oeuvre, which Csalagyi sees as an integral whole, with certain 'means of internal repetition, reenactments of individual registers of speaking', serving to integrate the different poetic genres employed by the poet over the years.[50] Important modes are the confessional, the portrayal of urban space in ways that evoke the visuality of cinema, the reoccurrence of dream-like states, as well as a kind of shared consciousness in a specific moment of time and space. The lyrical 'I' in Takács's work is not

---

46 Ibid., pp. 227–29.

47 Zoltán Szénási, 'Vallomás és szerep. Szalagyi Csilla Takács Zsuzsa költészete című könyvéről' [Confession and Role: On *The Poetry of Zsuzsa Takács* by Csilla Szalagyi], *Pannonhalmi Szemle* 30, no. 4 (2022), 116.

48 Csilla Szalagyi, *Takács Zsuzsa költészete* [The Poetry of Zsuzsa Takács] (Budapest: L'Harmattan Kiadó, 2022).

49 The monographs are: Ágnes Lehoczky, *Poetry, the Geometry of the Living Substance: Four Essays on Ágnes Nemes Nagy* (Cambridge: Cambridge Scholars Publishing, 2011); Halmai Tamás, *Gergely Ágnes* (Budapest: Balassi Kiadó, 2012); and Szalagyi, *Takács Zsuzsa költészete*.

50 Szénási, 'Vallomás és szerep', p. 118.

tied to one specific self (as is, for example, often the case in American confessional poetry), but assumes different roles.[51]

Csalagyi also remarks on the 'tragic, melancholic' tone of Takács' verse. In a 1997 essay about death in Hungarian poetry, Takács described a poem which she recalls her mother reciting to her—it might have turned up in a children's book in the 1920s—about three orphans crying to themselves in their abandoned, dark room, while their mother lies outside in the grave; the clumps of earth suddenly open up, the mother floats across the wild sky, her face pale, home towards her children . . . Takács mentions that she could not listen to this poem being recited without crying.[52] Csalagyi sees a dynamic counterpoint in the work of Takács between a tragic view, rooted in romanticism and the animating images in the lyrical tone of the work itself—the opposing poles of melancholy and hope.[53] In one interview, Takács stated that the 'dark irony' of writers such as Kafka and György Petri are cheering to her.[54]

In the final series of Takács poems in this anthology, the allegorical figure of Blind Hope appears in various settings, including a café, 'Last Judgement Square' in Budapest (an allegorical locale *par excellence*), including as well as the imaginary of Franz Kafka (Appellplatz, Kaffee Union). The figure of Blind Hope had appeared in a poem in an earlier volume of Takács', which the critic Tamás József Reményi had characterized as a kind of prayer in a state beyond faith, beyond belief, beyond hope. In the later cycle of poems, the feeling of lack is metaphorized,

---

51 Ibid.

52 Cited in Szalagyi, *Takács Zsuzsa költészete*, p. 21.

53 Ibid.

54 György Petri (1943–2000), Hungarian poet. In Zsuzsa Takács, 'A távollévő Isten mellett' [Zsuzsa Takács: Next to Distant God], interview with Lajos Jánossy, *Litera*, 1 September 2018: https://litera.hu/magazin/interju/takacsz-zsuzsa-megadom-magam-a-nalam-nagyobb-eronek.html (accessed 3 December 2025).

indicating an existential state of deprivation.[55] The way in which this deeply affecting cycle of poems is built upon, and yet crucially diverges from the (female) allegorical figure of 'treacherous, blind Hope!' contained in one of the verses of Enlightenment-era poet Mihály Csokonai Vitéz[56] itself bears witness to the transformative powers of Takács's creativity.

Zsófia Balla was born in Cluj-Napoca in 1949 to an assimilated Jewish family. Approximately one hundred members of her family, including her grandparents, whom she never met, were killed during the Holocaust. Her parents were deported to German death camps, returning home after the war. She studied violin in Cluj and received a teaching diploma from the Academy of Music in 1972. Her first volume of verse, *A dolgok emlékezete* [*The Memory of Things*] was published in 1968. Balla worked at the Hungarian section of the Cluj radio station until it was closed down in 1985. Between 1983 and 1989 she could not publish her work; she was also not allowed to leave Romania between 1980 and 1990. In 1993, Balla moved to Hungary, where she has lived ever since. Balla is the author of 17 volumes of poetry and nine works for the stage. She is the member of both the Széchenyi Academy of Letters and Arts and the Digital Literature Academy. Balla was awarded the Attila József Prize in 1996 and the Artisjus Literary Prize in 2010.

Several factors were crucial to Balla's development as a writer: of course, the overwhelming and inconceivable loss of most of her family in the genocide of the Second World War, but also her experience growing up as the member of the Hungarian (minority) community in Romania, and her training at music school. In many interviews, Balla has spoken in detail of the importance of all of these factors. Many critics have pointed to the musicality of her work, her familiarity with musical

---

55 Szalagyi, 'Vallomás és szerep', p. 210.

56 See 'Takács Zsuzsa: A távollévő Isten mellett'. Mihály Csokonai Vitéz (1773–1805), who was born and lived in Debrecen, was also an important predecessor to Szilárd Borbély, who devoted several studies and his Habilitation thesis to him.

genres, the use of such poetic forms as chanson and ballad. Balla has also spoken of the difficulties of existing as a minority language poet in Romania (in particular during the Ceaușescu years, 1965–1989), her decision to move to Hungary in 1993, and, although clearly drawn to Budapest as the centre of Hungarian literary life, having to rebuild one's life in a city bereft of the scents and sounds of childhood. In one interview, Balla described how, as a child, she would ask about her murdered grandparents:

> I tried to adopt many older aunties and uncles as my grandparents. I knew that I was Jewish from school, from the taunting of the other children. They didn't curse me, but at home I told my parents how the boys looked into the trousers of one of my classmates to see if he was circumcised. As a result of this examination, they began calling him a Christ-killer, a god-murderer. Those children . . . where had they gotten this, from whom had they heard it, we can ask this question . . . Then my mother told me the situation with our own Jewishness. I ran out into the corridor, and to the joy of all of the inhabitants of the building, I began yelling, in exaltation: 'I am a person three times over! I have Jewish heritage, Hungarian nationality, and I am a citizen of Romania!'—My mother ran after me, grabbed me, and dragged me back into the flat: 'I wasn't telling you to boast about it!'[57]

In the same interview, Balla discusses the origin of her artistic praxis:

> I have been writing ever since I was a child. I published my first poems when I was 16 years old, I began with that. My first volume, *The Memory of Things* [*A dolgok emlékezete*], was published in 1968, the year I graduated from high school . . . When I was 15 years old, stuck at home because my parotid glands were swollen, wandering around an elegant apartment in Brașov, I

57 'A költészet nyiliránya. Varga Melinda beszélgetés Balla Zsófiával' [The Direction of Poetry: A conversation between Melinda Varga and Zsófia Balla], *Irodalmi jelen*, 2 July 2018: https://irodalmijelen.hu/2018-jul-02-1707/-kolteszet-nyiliranya1 (accessed 3 December 2025).

> began to write about objects. At first, I only wanted to slip into their souls, to know what it meant to be a flower in a vase, the carpet beneath our feet, the ceiling above us, what it was like to be a whip or tulip. Then it seemed as if I could capture everything with poetry, as if was a butterfly net: a possible mummification, in other words to preserve the objects, to preserve living beings and moments, that is to say, to preserve ourselves within art.[58]

As the critic György Vári has expressed it:

> The memory of things abases, weighs upon you, and suffocates you, it cannot be overcome, therefore it must be transformed from memory into an idea, it must appear in poetry, as the exposition of existence itself, as a definition, and in this way it will no longer be degrading, it will become eternal, just as is indicated by the last picture, again and again, the gas burning every single day, as its own eternal flame, constant remembrance.[59]

In the words of the poet herself: 'Not only do things over and over again reminded me of the inconceivable, the unmeasurable. Absence itself is a memorial that is in motion, I am bumping into it all the time, like a door that keeps swinging back at me.'[60]

Of course, objects tend to be silent, and, as the critic Kitti Wölfinger points out, the positioning of Balla's oeuvre between *word and wordlessness, word and silence* points to a strong affinity with the work of both Ágnes Nemes Nagy and Zsuzsa Beney.[61] As Balla has commented: 'Nothing

---

58 Ibid.

59 György Vári, '"Van erre szó, de nincs emlékezet." Balla Zsófiáról' ['There is a Word for It, but No Memory.' On Zsófia Balla], *Holmi*, September 2007: https://www.holmi.org/2007/09/vari-gyorgy-van-erre-szo-de-nincs-emlekezet-jegyzetek (accessed 3 December 2025).

60 'A költészet nyilirány a'.

61 Kitti Wölfinger, 'Csillapulást találni a világban. Balla Zsófia költészetéről' [To Find Respite in the World: The Poetry of Zsófia Balla], *Korunk* 30, no. 7 (July 2019): 103–108.

can be kept silent forever, the earth throws its secrets out of itself. And not speaking, not knowing can never spare anyone from anything . . . One can only survive with knowledge and memory.'[62]

As Vári notes, the poem 'In the Other Wing of the Palace' stands at the edge of silence and words. The poet writes on gilt paper while the silence of a chorus 'circles in space, troubled'—writing, something solid and lasting, is contrasted to song and speech that has not yet began to sound. Speech is itself memory, and yet it is rendered mute by a weight as yet untransformed ('the thick lump of time / masses in the throat'). The image of the 'fishes howling' creates an acoustical impossibility (along with the paradox of the image of the water after the 'fire-warmth')—a metaphor for the antithesis of silence and the word. And yet the word is like a pearl that is born within this muteness, transforming the past into a memory-work (*emlék-mű*).[63]

Márton Szilágyi writes that at the centre of Balla's lyrical poetry there stands a subjectively open figure, a personality that exists through the 'repeated speaking of its own memories'. These memories open themselves up, in their details, to the experiential world and the world beyond it,[64] indicating, that, beyond the weight of things and memory, there might exist a glancing view of transcendence.

Zsuzsa Rakovszky was born in Sopron in 1950. Her father passed away when she was still a small child. She spent her school years in Sopron, then commenced her university studies in Debrecen, although she completed them at Eötvös Loránd University in Budapest, attaining a teaching diploma for Hungarian and English in 1975. After graduation, she worked as a librarian. Beginning in the 1980s, she began working as an editor, and from 1987 onward, as a freelance writer and translator. Her first book of poetry, titled *Jóslatok és határidők* [*Prophecies and Deadlines*], was published in 1981, although it was her second volume, *Tovább egy házzal* [*One House Later*], that brought her wide attention.

62 'A költészet nyilirányа'.

63 Vári, 'Van erre szó'.

64 Cited in Wölfinger, 'Csillapulást találni a világban', p. 106.

From the turn of the millennia, Rakovszky began writing prose as well, publishing several acclaimed novels. In 1990, she participated in the International Writing Program of the University of Iowa. Her poetry has been translated into English by George Szirtes (*New Life*, Oxford University Press, 1994), and her best-selling novel *Shadow of the Snake* has been translated into German, Italian, Bulgarian and Dutch. She has been awarded many prizes, including the Attila József Prize in 1988 and the Libri Literature prize in 2016. In 2009, she was made a member of the Széchenyi Academy of Literature and Arts.

Rakovszky grew up near the Austrian border, which, until 1989, was closed. Walls are a frequent reference in her work as a childhood experience. Because of the proximity of the border, special permission was required to travel internally to Sopron, and identities were often checked by soldiers in the forested areas. Rakovszky's memories of this time are of a tranquil, peaceful city, where the troubles of the adult world didn't really reach her, despite the early loss of her father.[65] As a small child, Rakovszky's mother read to her a great deal, including the great Hungarian Romantic ballads of János Vitez and Toldi.[66] To this day, Rakovszky resides in Sopron, an experience that is profoundly reflected in both her poetry and highly-regarded novelistic output.

As Beatrix Visy has noted, Rakovszky's poetry, lyrical in nature, is characterized by its rootedness in the 'thrownness' of existence (*Geworfenheit*, 'the state of being thrust into this world'), and the confrontation of human time and space with the infinite. Within space, time may become embodied, and within these spatialized forms, it gains

---

65 Tamás Dzsubák, 'Egy régi, lyukas felnőttpulóvert adtak rá, hogy nefázzon' [They Gave Her an Old, Threadbare Sweater So She Wouldn't Freeze], *Index*, 27 August 2023: https://index.hu/kultur/2023/08/27/rakovszky-zsuzsa-vita-elo-idoben/ (accessed 3 December 2025).

66 Discussion between Anna T. Szabó and Zsuzsa Rakovszky, 1 December 2020: https://www.youtube.com/watch?v=ofP0JDpHH44 (accessed 3 December 2025).

content and relations to other forms and objects.[67] To a certain degree, there is an object-centricity in Rakovszky's work which may remind one of the objects of both Ágnes Nemes Nagy and Zsófia Balla. Rakovszky's objects, though, are different in how they experience their own 'thrownness' into existence and into time—as well as their disintegration over time—with many of her poems documenting this phenomenon. Objects are catalogued within the lyric: 'Groceries and herring on a table, or / a deck of cards scattered round dimpled glass. / In a chilly blue-green dusk, huge wagons ford / a stream, bearing an inferior class / of cabbage' ('From the Dutch School', p. 238). These objects are also inevitably connected to the socialism of Hungary in the 1950s and 1960s, to Rakovszky's early years and the orchestrated scenery of life at that time: 'Mother's Day, Women's Day, Children's Day, Sports Day . . .' ('Decline and Fall', p. 239.) The many-layered palimpsest of recollection is made visible through the act of reconstituting these objects: 'a few / back numbers of a magazine called *New / Age*', a social Christian political magazine published in the late 1930s, and read by the 'old women of my childhood' (p. 242) evokes the remnants of the pre-Second-World-War years in Hungary coexisting with the 'Totalitarian-Classical, filthy terminals / in waiting rooms, provincial culture halls . . .'—referring to the neoclassical Stalinist architecture that became prevalent across the Eastern Bloc after 1948. The linearity of time itself is thrown into question—as occurs dramatically as well in poems such as 'Phantoms', the opening line of which states 'There is no past tense. The past isn't even past' (p. 246). The clashing of disparate historical periods can lead to a kind of absurdism or surrealism.

The inevitable dissent into ruin and obsolescence of the products of early socialism is a strong theme running through Rakovszky's earlier work, and the inevitable 'uselessness' of these objects may recall the

67 Beatrix Visy, 'Az idő és a tér csapdájában' [In the Snare of Time and Space], *Élet és irodalom* 47, no. 41 (13 October 2023): https://www.es.hu/cikk/2023-10-13/visy-beatrix/az-ido-es-a-ter-csapdajaban.html (accessed 3 December 2025).

analysis of Walter Benjamin: 'The other side of mass culture's hellish repetition of "the new" is a mortification of matter which is fashionable no longer.'[68] And yet these objects do not follow their trajectory in time alone—attached to them are fates, the fates of the 'small lives' of the provinces, whose narratives also form a major thread through Rakovszky's oeuvre, and which may put one in mind of the 'small fates' of Teju Cole (although clearly in a very different context). Originally inspired by the journalistic genre of *faits divers*, 'a French innovation, used in newspapers for over a century, that translates to "incidents" or "various things" or just "fillers"', Cole's 'small fates' are, in fact, brief recapitulations of dramatic events in the domestic lives of Lagosians.[69] Roland Barthes defined *faits divers* as 'disasters, murders, rapes, accidents, thefts, all this refers to man, to his history, his alienation, his hallucinations, his dreams, his fears.'[70]

Whereas Cole drew his inspiration for his 'small fates' from the reportage of dramatic events in the newspapers of Lagos, Rakovszky has found at least part of her inspiration in photographic ekphrasis, based upon the massive online publicly-sourced photographic archive known as Fortepan,[71] originally created in 2010 as a website to host found photographs of Budapest but now including locations even outside of Hungary (the poem on p. 258, 'Forest', is taken from the 'Fortepan' series).[72] Indeed many poems in Rakovszky's oeuvre evoke the 'history, alienation, hallucinations, dreams [and] fears' of the citizens of the provinces, particularly during the years following 1989; as George Szirtes puts it: 'The world of [Rakovszky's] poems is recognizably the

---

68 Susan Buck-Morss, *The Dialectics of Seeing: Walter Benjamin and the Arcades Project* (Cambridge and London: The MIT Press, 1991), p. 159.

69 Cited in Macy Halford, 'Teju Cole's Small Fates', *The New Yorker*, 17 August 17 2011.

70 Ibid.

71 Originally a manufacturer of film products, the Kodak firm Forte was sold to a Hungarian bank in 1947, and subsequently nationalized in 1948, its products renamed 'Fortepan.' It ceased production in 2001.

72 More recent poems engage in 'traditional' ekphrasis as well, based upon paintings by Rembrandt and Tivadar Csontváry Kosztka (see pp. 264 and 266).

world of her readers, the shifting urban landscape of noisy neighbours, malfunctioning television sets, shadows on landings, snatched meetings, and dying ideologies.'[73] The poem 'In an Alpha State' (p. 252) is particularly evocative of Hungary in the 1990s, with four individuals, identified only by their initials B., C., D., and G., casting about to find a path through life after 'regime change'—B. can't get reimbursed by his insurance company, C. is being defrauded by a contractor, D. is trying to sell organic groceries on the web, and D. falsifies sell-by dates on ketchup bottles. They seek group spiritual inquiry as a guide through the chaos, but end up even more displaced in time, as they share their visions afterwards, some of which border on the biblical ("The narrow walls beat back the rumbling of God'), others on the ironically absurd: 'I saw a woman swear allegiance / to a microwave. My own mother became / a fire hydrant.' Szilárd Borbély associates the 'concealment of the Name' of the personages in Rakovszky's poetry, employing the archaic practice of presenting the individual and their 'masking', with the medieval and allegorical poetic form of the Danse Macabre.[74] The invocation of the 'political hopelessness' of the decade following 'regime change' demonstrates a strong affinity with the poetry of György Petri as well.

Many of these poems are hunted by the uncanny, the Unheimlich, in which the boundaries between everyday life and the spectres of the past are more than negotiable: these spectres can breach the frail membrane of the present at any time. In 'Phantoms', a soldier from a war that ended decades ago drives a tank towards one of the poem's narrators whose car just crashed on a moonlit country road, having completed a routine errand. In many regards, this intrusion of the not-so-distant past (Hungary during the Second World War) into the empty post-1989, post-liberal present takes merely one step further the absurd clash

73 Zsuzsa Rakovszky, *New Life* (George Szirtes trans.) (Oxford: Oxford University Press, 1994), p. vii.

74 Szilárd Borbély, *Hungarikum-e a líra? Esszék, kritikák* [Is Lyrical Poetry Hungarian? Essays and Criticism] (Budapest: Parnasszus Könyvek-Magasles, 2012), pp. 110–11.

of epochs, the jarring historical patchwork of discontinuity that has defined life in central Europe over the past century and longer (the only exception being the ever-present 'politics of forgetting', a politics of which these poems could be said to form a subtle and ironic critique).

Much of Rakovszky's work posits the poem as a haunting, the poem as hauntology, drawing us to the multi-layered palimpsest of the past through the word, the 'presence made of absence',[75] a lyrical intervention reminding us that, surrounded by the detritus of a 'past and useless age', its material objects, and the people who held those objects in their hands, yet exist on another plane continually intersecting with ours.

Krisztina Tóth, born in Budapest 1967, studied sculpture at the Vocational High School of Fine and Applied Arts, graduating in 1986. Subsequently, she worked as an intern in the National Museum. She enrolled at the Faculty of Arts at Eötvös Loránd University, spending a study period in Paris, where she began translating French poetry. She completed her university degree in Hungarian in 1992, and began working at the Budapest French Institute in 1994. From 1998 onward, she has been a freelance writer. Tóth has published nine volumes of poetry, 11 volumes of prose, and dozens of books for children. Her work has been translated into 18 languages, and she is the recipient of numerous literary prizes, including the Artisjus Literature prize in 2010, and the Alföld Prize in 2014. Her novel *Eye of the Monkey* [*A majom szeme*][76] was a bestseller in Hungary in 2022.

As George Szirtes notes in his introduction to his translations of Krisztina Tóth's poems,[77] 'It would be great mistake to project the embodiment of a social or political crisis on to specific individuals, especially writers, and perhaps most of all, poets. Poets are not sociologists.

---

75 Cited in Sadeq Rahimi, *The Hauntology of Everyday Life* (Cham: Palgrave Macmillan, 2021), p. 12.

76 Krisztina Tóth, *Eye of the Monkey* (Ottilie Mulzet trans.) (New York: Seven Stories Press, 2025).

77 Krisztina Tóth, *My Secret Life: Selected Poems* (George Szirtes trans.) (Hexham: Bloodaxe Books, 2025).

They respond to the extraordinary complexities of their lives and the lives around them and all the various instinctive dimensions open to each one of them individually.'[78] And yet, just as the poets born earlier in the twentieth century were forced to deal with the traumas of the Second World War and its aftermath in Hungary, Tóth—as was the case with many of her contemporaries—inevitably found herself forced to deal with the rather chaotic circumstances that ensued in Hungary in the 1990s after the sudden, unexpected cessation of late communist rule referred to not as revolution, as in the case of Czechoslovakia, but as 'regime change'.

As Szirtes notes, Tóth's first prize-winning book of poems was published in 1989, the year of the great changes.[79] It is difficult not to see at least some of the profound disillusionment associated with the failed promises of 1989—the onset of massive corruption, the aggressive monetization of so many aspects of life, the non-transparent privatization of state enterprises, and, as Szirtes comments, the rupture of many personal relationships due to political reasons (perhaps no less affected by the onset of 'wild east' capitalism and the new scarcity of time)—as informing Tóth's subsequent oeuvre, both in prose and poetry. Tóth clearly hails from the tradition that encompassed both the early twentieth century literary movement known as *Nyugat* (West), and subsequently, *Újhold*,[80] particularly (I feel) in the ethical mandate of both movements. While it is true that Tóth's work is characterized by a certain 'obscurity/uncertainty (dream-like states)', as Viktória Radics points out, it also contains 'hyper-realistic details'[81] that point with extreme specificity to everyday life in post-communist Hungary. The musicality of Toth's verse, as well as its formal perfection (including the use of colloquial elements of speech),

78 Ibid., p. 12.

79 Ibid., p. 11.

80 Viktória Radics, 'Emberruhában' [In Human Attire], *Holmi* 22, no. 11 (November 2010), p. 1477.

81 Ibid., p. 1475.

mean that the *otherness* (to use Radics' term) portrayed in her work is even more eerie.

Tóth's creativity is vast, and includes her achievements as an accomplished stained-glass artist (she completed training in applied arts when younger and for a while supported herself through her stained-glass creations), as well as being a prolific translator of over 20 volumes from French. Like the fleeting play of briefly glimpsed lights and reflections in glass, Tóth's poems remain apart from epic narrative, or even the monumental abstraction of Nemes Nagy's 'objective lyricism'. Rather, they form delicate, exquisite miniatures in which seemingly banal instances of middle-class European daily life in the early third millennium are infused with sudden twists of meaning, at times gaining almost mystical significance, as in the poem 'Shadowgrass' on p. 273, which begins with the everyday act of untangling an extension cord to mow the lawn and ends with an invocation for the grass in the yard to grow as high as the sky. Other everyday images are enveloped still further in a pervasive sense of the Surrealist shock of recognition and the startling uncanniness of the Unheimlich, as in 'Vatera' (p. 291), in which the narrator describes browsing an online second-hand market for a doll for her young daughter: 'I bid for it but was outbid by someone / who wanted a little girl with a terrified face, / a four-foot-three high silicone woman / wearing knee-socks and sandals', echoing, among other objects, the series of grotesque dolls La Poupée created by the surrealist artist Hans Bellmer.

Surrealism equally operated upon the creative principle of the inclusion of the random, the accidental, in other words the elements outside of immediate (conscious) authorial control and planning. As can be inferred from more than one interview, Tóth clearly makes chance one of the guiding principles for literary creation: an unexpected sighting, overheard fragments of speech, or personal encounter often forms the seed from which the poem germinates. An action as banal as leaving a message on an answering machine can be transformed into a liturgy of grief with its obsessive repetitions ('Machine Voice', p. 278).

Yet any discussion of Tóth's work, unfortunately, cannot remain unaffected by the circumstances of her life even in the (semi-)open society of contemporary Hungary. For one, the matter of personal appearance before the male gaze, even within critical writing. If Ágnes Nemes Nagy has often been mentioned in terms of her physical beauty, Tóth in turn faced, in at least one early essay discussing her literary work, an observation on her 'attractive exterior'. More saliently (and recently), after Tóth commented, in an online literary magazine in 2021, that perhaps two 'classics' in the national literature curriculum should be exchanged for books that represent more positive gender roles for girls, a campaign of cyberbullying and cyberhate followed, including harassment in the street where Tóth resided in Budapest and excrement dumped in her mailbox.[82] She and her family, including her adopted daughter of Roma origin, were obliged to relocate abroad. The enormous price Tóth has paid for speaking up about gender issues in Hungary—even within the scope of a number of questions posed by an online literary magazine—is a deeply distressing statement on the state of gender equality in Hungary today.

In her essay 'The Nameless Ones', Ágnes Nemes Nagy wrote:

> The poet is the expert of feelings. While practising my profession, I have often felt that these so-called feelings are composed of at least two layers. The first layer carries feelings known to us and recognizable; and they have names: joy, terror, love, offense. (For the most part their meanings are commonly defined, they have a past, they have been studied, they have a literary history). They are the citizens of our heart. The second layer is the no-man's-land of the nameless ones . . . I believe that one of the poet's obligations is to try to obtain citizenship for as many of the Nameless Ones as possible.[83]

82 See 'HLO in Support of Krisztina Tóth', *Hungarian Literature Online*: https://hlo.hu/news/hlo-in-support-of-krisztina-toth.html (accessed 18 November 2025).

83 Ágnes Nemes Nagy, *Szó és szótlanság: Összegyűjtött esszék I* [Word and Wordlessness: Collected Essays] (Budapest: Magvető Kiadó, 1989), p. 533.

Tóth's work collects these 'nameless ones'—perhaps digging even deeper than her predecessor might have anticipated, into realms that include the underside of life, relationships, the body, the urban milieu of Pest—while illuminating their underground existence with profound lyrical beauty.

Anna T. Szabó, born in Cluj-Napoca in 1972, is the third poet in this volume to hail from Romania, moving with her family to Hungary in 1987. Szabó received a teacher's diploma from Eötvös Loránd University in 1997, subsequent to which she completed her PhD in the English Renaissance and Baroque. She has translated the work of Shakespeare, James Joyce, Sylvia Plath, Beatrix Potter and W. B. Yeats. Szabó began publishing her work during her university studies; since 1995, she has published five volumes of poetry, four children's books and several volumes of prose. Szabó has received numerous literary prizes and honours, including the Tibor Déry Prize, and the Akademie der Künste Berlin–Junge Akademie stipend.

Szabó attended school in Cluj-Napoca until 1987. Her childhood was deeply connected to poetry: she received her first book of verse (*Ha a világ rigó lenne* [If the World Were a Thrush] by Sándor Weöres) when she was only one year old.[84] In an interview, Szabó speaks of how the most fundamental rhyming elements in her work come from the children's rhymes she heard spoken by her grandmother, who hailed from Vlaha (Magyarfenes) in Romania. 'I have an elemental relationship to poetry, stemming from my childhood,' Szabó commented: 'Someone might have written some foolish rhyme, incomprehensible and strange, and it still affects me: many years later I'm sitting in the car driving somewhere, and it comes into my mind, maybe as a way of self-torture, because clearly I have a bad conscience, that I'm too late. From this elemental joy

---

84 Anna T. Szabó, 'Nekem az örömön kívül semmi sem egyértelmű a világban' [Except for Joy, Nothing in This World Is Straightforward for Me], interview with Domi Milanovich, *WMN*, 30 June 2022: https://wmn.hu/kult/57882-szabo-t-anna-nekem-az-oromon-kivul-semmi-sem-egyertelmu-a-vilagban (accessed 3 December 2025).

of words, I can easily end up in a madness of words, perhaps these two things are the same. Perhaps joy is merely some kind of vagary.'[85] This profound joy in the Hungarian language, its repertoire of sounds and rhythms, is found everywhere in Szabó's work (with a musicality surely as masterful as that of Weöres); to cite only one example, her deft use of the ballad form is devastatingly and subversively employed in the poem 'Persephone' (p. 329), which retells the classic myth from the point of view of a working-class woman. Szabó also speaks of the 'tactile euphoria' of verse, and how the experience of reciting a poem by Sándor Weöres with a group of young schoolchildren in a tiny village restores her faith in poetry.[86] (Szabó, like Krisztina Tóth, makes frequent educational visits to Hungarian classrooms.)

Anna T. Szabó is perhaps one of the first poets to write about motherhood in a deeply visceral sense—both physically and psychically—including the process of labour and birth and the ambivalence of motherhood ('Delivery Room', p. 320), a somewhat taboo subject even today, acknowledging the betrayal within the paradigm of motherly love. Her poem 'Woman on a Plaid Blanket' (p. 328) dissects the so-called 'male gaze' with distance and irony, but driving home the point of how it empties women of subjectivity: 'So that's what I am / when I'm not here.'

Sasha Dugdale writes:

> But although Szabó writes compellingly about motherhood, her poetry extends to embrace the wider experience of women, their slow acts of disappearance, their cultural and existential elision. I'm fascinated by her charting of that moment when a woman is faced with a sudden realization that she is not a man in a male world, that the train is pulling away without her, the men have gone and she is left with her loneliness and bloodstains—and that she is and always will be an outsider, even in her own dreams and imaginative play. There is a point in the writing of every woman poet with the ambition to be truthful to her voice,

85 Ibid.

86 Ibid.

at which becomes abundantly clear that she cannot write with the voice of her literary predecessors, because they wrote from an entirely different place, and of a different life experience, and she must strike out on her own. This can be unpleasant and lonely . . . Subversion of genre, of material and voice, has infinite possibilities for those with this understanding. It is a way of entering the canon under cover of night and robbing it of its treasures.[87]

The final poem in this anthology, Szabó's 'Protocol' (p. 332), is about her paternal grandmother, more specifically helping her with her bath when the poet was only 23, about to be married, and her grandmother 80 years of age. The poem remarks on the medicalization of death in the modern age ('the cold white cloak / in which specialists of the body pass / uniformed like angels'), the contrast between her grandmother's body and her own, but cumulates in the poet's own forced confrontation with her grandmother's body as viewed in the clinical language of the medical report, likened to 'an alien hand in a rubber glove / [that] grabs my heart and throws it on the scales.' The cold clinical language is crushing, and yet the poet is able to speak the experience, surely a form of triumph.

The connection the poet feels to her grandmother is like a living emblem of our own connections to our own mothers, to our grandmothers, our poet-mothers and our poet-forebears. The lines of affinity throughout this volume leading from poet to poet, crisscrossing generations and lives, are also a part of this.

*

It has been a profound privilege to sit with the words and presences of these women. Their lives and their work are like maps—intellectual, spiritual, psychological—that can guide us through our own age, as they

87 Sasha Dugdale, Introduction to Anna T. Szabó, *Trust* (Claire Pollard with Anna T. Szabó trans) (Todmorden: Arc Publications, 2021), p. 12.

were and have been forced to confront their own ambiguous and uncertain place within Hungarian history and the Hungarian literary world—a milieu that at times, it seems, has granted them at best grudging acceptance. And yet I would never think of reducing any of this work to any kind of utilitarian purpose, only that the work of all these women has been like a signpost in my own life, a message of survival, not only physical, but in the most profound psychic and spiritual sense of the word. Perhaps that is the most important message they convey to us: to see the burdens they, as women, have had to carry, and yet they found the strength within themselves to create within the bounds of a language that does not always welcome them with open arms. Perhaps the poetic writing of these women can be considered to be a kind of minor language, in the sense that Deleuze and Guattari used the term, in the ways in which a *minor language* can subvert the means and the ends of the majoritarian context in which it occurs.[88] In any event, in editing this collection, I have only wanted to bring together, to convey within English, the work of a number of poets whose oeuvre I find to be of outstanding, life-giving importance. My sole wish for this anthology is for it to stand as an homage to these women and their exceptional artistry.

Ottilie Mulzet

Prague

17 November 2025

---

88 See Gilles Delueze and Felix Guattari, *Kafka: Toward a Minor Literature* (Dana Polan trans.) (Minneapolis: University of Minnesota Press, 1986).

ÁGNES NEMES NAGY

(1922–1991)

TREES

It's time to learn. The winter trees.
How head to toe they're clad in frost.
Stiff monumental tapestries.

It's time to learn that region where
the crystal turns to steam and air,
and where the trees swim through the mist
like something remembered but long lost.

The trees, and then the stream behind,
the wild duck's silent sway of wing,
the deep blue night, white and blind,
where stand the hooded tribe of things,
here one must learn the unsung deeds
of heroism of the trees.

Translated by George Szirtes

FEMALE LANDSCAPE

A lie of land so yielding, gentle,
you want to stroke it, see it break.
Between its knees the broad stream flows
glittering like a curious snake.

Dense valley, luxuriant hill
gentled under aeons of praise—
this female landscape loses me:
what can I do but stand and gaze?

The Baltic Sea has bathed her feet,
Tyrrhenian foam has washed her hair,
but her smooth naval makes me think
of quite another place, elsewhere,

where tortoises are being taught,
where life grows taller and the dim
heat sucks scarlet flowers from
the giant spiky cactus limb,

where children ride mosquitoes,
where neither light nor reed is blunt,
where all is bladed as the mind,
and hot as any hothouse plant,

where honey-thick, yet thicker still,
juice drips down the moss of trees,
and in the pond cool greenish stars
pulse against my calves and knees,

where the lobster slops and burrows
through mud hotter than any mud,
and thought flowers from my shoulder
with its stout unfurling bud.

Translated by George Szirtes

JOURNAL (SELECTIONS)

MIND

I know I have no reasonable grounds
for thinking, but watch the thoughts as they go round.
And since contempt's appropriate to the act
mindlessly I trust to intellect.

NIGHTMARE

From a world of rotting rags and clout
the marsh-light of cold reason flashes out,
plays on the corpse, the softening skull beneath,
and illuminates its naked row of teeth.

REVENGE

He who cannot take revenge,
nor yet forgive, must find redress
in burning forever the low flame
of his unquenchable bitterness.

SIE ITUR AD ASTRA

Compare with these I am a saint
            no judge would dare try me;
if the world wags on like this
            they will deify me.

JULY 1

Light and light and sunspots, fragrant colours,
in place of my heart, *de rigueur*—bouquets.
Just this once, dear world, I will forgive you,
but from now on you'll have to mend your ways!

YOU SIT AND READ

You sit and you read. How alone you are, even you don't know.
But sometimes you guess and then with a leisurely movement
and a hint of mild animal sadness, your simple features
dip into the light.

BEFORE THE MIRROR

You take your face and slowly remove the paint,
but would remove the face that fate assigned you,
you wait for the armchair to rise and with a faint
gesture of boredom to appear behind you.

CONTEMPLATIVE

The old pose lost its charm. Let's take
a new one out. Yes, this will do.
In matters of dress it's all the same
what you fit your body to.

The dress, the body and the soul,
the same applies to everything.
When Thespis prinks does she at all
suspect what change the colours bring?

SINCERITY

Inspecting myself makes me bilious.
It's easier for the spontaneous.
I would if I could be the driver of the dray
who washes great blonde horses all the day
and has nothing to say.

Translated by George Szirtes

BETWEEN

The air's enormous empty sleeves.
Air supporting birds and the whole panoply
of bird-lore, ornithology,
wings on fraying winds of argument,
the unpredictable, inconsequent
boughs that a moment of sky relieves,
trees of living mist, spiralling desire
to the topmost branches,
breathing, twenty to a minute at a time,
vast angels barnacled in rime.

The mass below. The plain with mounds
of earth, juddering, huge, immovable,
where ridges and hump-backed cliffs lie down
or kneel—geography's sculpture hall—
the vale a moment of forgetfulness where
attention wanders, and then more
masses and forms from skeletons of lime bone
to the far perimeter, a single core
of being, crumpled into stone.

Between the earth and sky.

Explosions in deep mountain bores.
Meanwhile the sun's transparent ores

turn stone to metal, almost to themselves,
and when beasts walk across them, their claws smoke,
and smoke-ribbons of burning hoofs
wind round and round above the cliffs' sheer roofs,
till night falls on the desert plain,
night that quenches and extends into the tight
core of what was stone, sub-zero night,
among the splitting and collapsing
of cartilage, joint, flagstone, sett,
flexed in an endless
decimating unconsciousness
by white and black quotidian
lightning flashes without sound—
Between the day and night.

Those decimations and incisions,
droughts and visions,
inarticulate resurrections,
the unbearable vertical tensions
between up-above and down-below—

Various climates and conditions.
Between. The stone. The tracks of tanks.
A line of black reed on savannah border,
written on pond and sky in lines, in double order,
two dark stones with cryptographs
stars' diacritics, acutes and graves—

Between sky and sky.

Translated by George Szirtes

STATUES

Bitter.
Bitter the ocean when I rolled
down the cliff's throat, a pebble stumbling
down spiral stairs, and as I fell
I heard the empty shell,
like memory in an empty house behind me humming,
and I rattled
like loose metal, shrapnel in the skull.

Then tumbled out across the beach
to find the statues.

There, on a sculpted base
a turtle's egg with its own carapace:
my skull simmering in heat of day,
my white helmet rolled away,
a tiny bubble in the sand,
I lay, my shoulders against the cliff's broad foot
filthy, filthy in my stained white suit.

Whose is this block?
Who was it who from this mountain of slate
furiously carved an extraordinary state
of indifference out of rock?

And tin, small shards of tin all over me,
buckled tin cans, metal panes
that, stuttering, beat back the light,
brilliant as the wreck of a downed plane,
something still living moving within,
a watchstrap, bloodstained,
I lay there spread against the cliff
an animated filth laid over stone.

No one more stubborn than you, none,
you who cast yourself in stone
into object, into stone
your live neck and backbone
this is an age of stone, an age,
a blind life of diminished sense.

Who carved out such indifference?
Who was it carved that living weight
of neck out of this heap of slate?

Salt and sand, the mass of rock above,
cave carved in sky,
this relative eternity
these minerals in twilight dress—

the sea booms out, one Earth its bed:
a stone bowl for its bitterness.

Translated by George Szirtes

STATUES I CARRIED

Statues I carried on board,
vast faces unnamed and unspanned.
Statues I carried on board
to the island where they should stand.
Between nose and ear there were ninety
degrees, measured precisely,
with no other sign of their rank.
Statues I carried on board,
and so I sank.

Translated by George Szirtes

LAZARUS

As slowly he sat up, the ache suffused
his whole left shoulder where his life lay bruised,
tearing his death away like gauze, section by section.
Since that is all there is to resurrection.

Translated by George Szirtes

REVENANT

This was the table. Legs and board.
This was the wire. This the lamp.
A glass beside it. Here it is.
The very water that I drank.

From this window I looked out
and saw the crooked dripping mist,
a huge branch in the darkening pool
of the field like a limp wrist.
I looked from the window in the wall
and I had eyes and arms and all.

I'm like a chair leg now, so tall.
I seem to kneel, so low am I
who cut through space once, shoulder high.
How many birds there were. What space.
Like flowers in a windswept lace
of fire, their petals torn, that sway
and hiss in swarms, or float away
at one great throb and spring apart
like fragments of a bird's blown heart.
There's one explosion and they fly.
And that was fire. And that was sky.

I'm going now. I would
reach to the ceiling if I could.
A low draught blowing where I list
out in the street. I don't exist.

Translated by George Szirtes

TO A SLEEPING FIGURE

You, anonymous, bare figure,
you who rise from every heap
of silent ash, you occupy
the seventh chamber with your sleep,

not dead but sleeping in your bed
of bark beside an ash-grey wall:
within the room torn curtains fall,
their great unmoving wings outspread.

I do not stir.
Mere states revolve, slow inundations:
sleep images alone remain
turning in unseen constellations.

Wake up! Wake up! Thrust shoulders free.
Though wounded almost mortally
I'll find you yet and talk life out.
Speak, tell me where you've been at last
in dreams you cannot speak about.

Translated by George Szirtes

FROM THE NOTEBOOKS OF AKHENATON

There must be something I could bring
to bear on this long suffering,
some deity I could invent,
to sit aloft, omniscient.

Desire's no longer adequate:
heaven should be of rough cement.
Therefore, lord, I'll take your weight
and raise you to the firmament
where cherubs will maintain your state.
Once you're up I'll see you right:
you'll not go naked in the night.
Now go and clip this bloody track
of griefs about your waiting neck,
and let it be the lukewarm robe you wear
(your tender plants have ever been my care).
And seal my search for truth behind the doors
of that jewel-encrusted heart of yours.

Enough. Proclaim how good it is,
perform your mighty offices,
sit, stare, eternally, in state.
Begin, it is already late.

Translated by George Szirtes

THE NIGHT OF AKHENATON

By the time he reached the open square that night
the tents had been soaked through with lanternlight,
candles were stuck in bottles. It was bright
as summer on this All Souls Day,
and on improvised shelves there lay
crepe-paper dolls of rose pink thick with dust.

Piled up on one side were tattooed heaps
of oil green melon rinds, their bodies scarred
with heart shapes picked out with old knitting needles.
Above them, neon signs were curling like hair.
A hot wind. Straw in the air.
The night was very dark.

He walked, as if circumscribed
by his presence in some guise,
walked without moving, as a train ran by
on rails above him.

Wash your face now. Dip your face
in the bowl of your cupped palms,
in the basin of your palms
the will is most where it is least,
let it drink like a bird,
let it drink, like beast,
wash your face now, let the sun,

each of whose beams terminates
in one small hand, oh let it run
its hands across your face—

Night now. And the canvas, growing heavier,
slumped between the pools of light,
between the stalls, which sparkled like boiled sweets
and hung like distant glow-worms, gleaming,
candles suffocated: sudden gusts.

The old garden.
Hundreds of thousands in the garden,
under a sky the colour of wafer,
it's the other face that must be swallowed,
and the green flower, the Judas tree
he hangs himself on in disgrace,
and the faint green of a star above,
the infinite walked in the garden,
I only wish that you, my love
were as small as the god on the wafer.

And the tanks were already coming.
The street ran along
its stone bed before mountainous waves of metal,
and soft bodies ran between stone and metal
still trailing a few balloons behind them,
their flapping canvas of collapsing tents,
the splashing sound of barriers,
distant ashes and fine showers of glass,
and in the silences, whatever blew above them,
whatever blew
above, above the entire planet.
He leapt across some rails along
with all the others,

together they rolled down an embankment,
piecemeal, jerkily, tumbled
under continuous gunfire, over each other
like an avalanche.

*

There was fog by the time he could see again.
He lay on the embankment. A reed.
Another body beside him in the mud,
stretched out so cool, so any old how
you'd think the fresh snow were intended for him.
He left him lying. With a single movement
he rose up, as if he were smoke,
left him lying, or rose up from within him,
and he looked so transparent lying there.
He rose, he lay, it was a single movement.

And was still carrying him, even as he set off.
Still carried the body in the dreaming light.
Through horizontal lines of attenuated mist
he went,
his left hand wrapped up in his right.

Translated by George Szirtes

AKHENATON IN HEAVEN

There everything is as it is. The mine.
A mountainside cleft to its heel. The instruments.
As he gently taps the limestone face
dawn shakes, uncertain of its place.
As if it were dawning from within,
the whole cliff like a narrow sheet,
stone and iron transparent now and thin
after ultimate defeat.

There lies the forest.
The fog proceeds in chunks.
Five-fingered, like abandoned hands,
or stretching upward, vertical,
they're tugged along as if by hawsers,
and, failing to gain a meaningful stature, are found
trickling faintly along the ground,
so they proceed,
and so expand or fall in broken ranks,
cloudy, attenuated trunks,
an alternative forest moving between the trees,
billowing mock boughs and shrubberies.

A tunnel there under the trees.
Shady grasses, gravel:
a narrowgauge railway, and now daybreak.

The sun arriving on a head of steam,
slicing the fog neatly, beam by beam,
sun on its way, as its mute rumbling shows,
the metal under the grass sparkles and glows,
the whole morning glows,
while a wall of bushes suddenly rises up,

where the rails have stopped under their grassy bed.
Then only a few sleepers lie ahead,
like halting steps to be negotiated,
and clearing where the sun stops dead.

It's morning there. Enormous plants.
The camomile field still and solemn,
hoarding a few scraps of iron,
the air above them thick with pollen,
the white spokes of vegetative suns,
unruffled galaxies, no wind whatever.
Noon. For eternity. For ever.

Translated by George Szirtes

THE OBJECTS

Look up to their massed blocks. In noon light they stand, apart.
The objects are at peace within my heart.

ABOVE THE OBJECT

Because the head of every object glows,
trees glisten like arctic circles. In long rows
all 92 elements stand, frozen in endless white,
each wearing its own curious cap of light,
on each one's brow its likeness and reflection—
so body, I trust, shall rise in resurrection.

Translated by George Szirtes

NIGHT OAK

Night-time: the walker,
hearing a sound, turned round to see
an oak tree in pursuit.

Stopped and waited for it. The oak
proceeded dragging on raw roots
still shedding earth, wriggling long serpentine limbs
down the metalled road,
an awkward mermaid thrusting forward,
its crown too broad, brushing against
silent awnings,
and having reached the night walker
it stopped to lean against the lamp post,
push hair aside.
Behind the hair an oak tree's face looked out.

Huge face of moss. Perhaps. Or something like.
The night walker felt his own
contours grow slack,
his dissolving coastline swimming in fog,
like one darkening
in a hidden tarn in a forest,
this was the face he reflected.

Both paused, took breath.

There were birds' nests in the oak's hair,
and in them, sleeping birds, unaware
unremembered.
                                        Because the matter was urgent.
It stood there motionless and urgent
like a news item in oak form,
which stales, uninterpreted.

Let fall its curtain of hair.
Turned round. Set off. Strange footed.

It took its nests and birds
and before the solidifying eyes
of the night walker
neon signs sprinkled light on it,
and melted back into the hole in the ground
which was ready to receive it.

Translated by George Szirtes

FOUR PANES OF GLASS

1

The first is a park.
A garden path between leafless branches,
a garden path, a thick yew tree one side
dotted with tiny winter fruit
glazed *fin-de-siècle* red
and other things,
more details yet—but why?
It is the garden path that marks
this pane, the path like a bird's neck
whose backward arch may be conveyed
by using hands, not words,
stretching its inconceivable avian head
towards the fogged density of the garden.

2

The second pane is misted.

3

The third pane is concrete.
I mean a garage roof
(one sliced in half by the sill, and below it,
invisible, in made to measure
tarpaulin, a selection of creatures,

retracting the lightnings of their lacquered,
polished, chrome surfaces,
hollow cylinders
of silent four-stroke machines
in the viscous chill of winter garages)
and outside, scalding winter suns,
the spotted woodpecker's tropical
spectra caught in the wrong climate,
as it crosses the snowfield
and rounds the horizon
like a steering wheel, spinning
noon rings about the flashing sun.

4

The fourth pane is sky,
stretched tight, without creases.
The rare silence of the atmosphere
as it fails to write on thick slate
its inexhaustible cloud dialogue,
one or two lines, no more, broken signs,
attempts at interpretation,
shred, constituent, promise.

Translated by George Szirtes

SPECTACLE

The blue. The green. The bed of the stream.
The way things change.
The walls of my skull are plastered with images
like a circular screen.

Even by night they disturb me,
the walls with their night-luminosity,
their bright knives, furniture—
a fern shakes me awake as I lie
with its long-rotted underside
and spores,
like an aerial photograph
of complex city floors—

They're sharp all right, yes, sharp,
every image perfectly sharp,
I'm blinded by the way they mass in herds
coming and going in silence,
tin and grease and birds
in flight without dimension,
planets without electron shields
driven to high densities,
roots mangled into balls
as they spin infinitely far from us

trapped in an incandescent present
in spaces without intervals.

I live in a tree.
                                        bough has no seasons,
it touches the sky and almost stutters.
I see crowds of husked fruit
gathering.

Translated by George Szirtes

THE TRANSFORMATION OF A RAILWAY STATION

Unlikely,

that there should be earth under all this, here where cobblestones clad the street like prehistoric fossils. But it seems that under the stones, under the cables, under the intricate lymphatic system (those pulsing installations) there is earth after all, despite everything: there is earth.

A crater now, as it turns out. Or a major surgical incision. On a large rare beast from the zoo, with anaesthetic and outsize instruments. Intestines piled high. Because this body must be dissected, lobe by lobe. The liver and kidneys are separated out. Brutal yet precise movements, half way between butchery and healing.

The incision area is sensitive. Tortured houses with peeling stucco, like secondary symptoms of disease. Exhausted trams lurch down ligatured veins, connections tacked together over a shortage of subsiding stones, swollen stitches of rail. And the plants, those ultimately defenceless beings whose stalks they break when they throw them in the bin, as they broke Christ's limbs after taking him off the cross: the dusty terror of plants.

In the middle of all this, the excavation. Diggers with fixed platforms. The operator above like a pilot suspended in mid-air. The astronauts in lemon-yellow rubbers clambering into ditches. Between barriers, the ear-splitting racket, the studied calm of catastrophe, the panic of indifference. A plastic bag covering a tangle of wires. (The food packages of the world. Paper, plastics, the odd piece of waterproof canvas. Textures, knots, dressings. Behold this, oh lordlings, behold that, behold the other.) And some pretty strange hats! A whaler's sou'wester, some form of ritual mask.

Here, we will establish an institutional headquarters. Here, the main hall. Asparagus goes here, notice board there. Look . . . can you see? Up there, among all those vacant cubic metres, there, yes there, that is where we shall put whatever does not yet exist. It's still transparent, still negotiable. It's a bit draughty up there. A good lens can fix that though. And the appropriate wattage. For it's the merest whisker that forms the barrier between it and ourselves, the merest whisker that prevents it existing. You can practically see its edges above you, hovering between certainty and uncertainty, so it is almost ready to be discussed as it swims into your ken like something diminishing put into reverse (a huge hazy ocean liner), pre-existent with all its impenetrable storeys.

You do, of course, remember the railway turntable? The station terminated in an elliptical foundation stone, and at the head of the foundation stone, the steel drum. The engine was parked on it and turned with it like a circus elephant. The old yellow station building is still there with its ancient but still-functioning nostalgias. The lamps behind curls of steam, the dawn rain. And the rails and sleepers at night (you must look at these from above, from the bridge). Those crepuscular angelic ladders into horizontal infinity.

But turn around. Take another look at the building site. (What I mean is that you should try to find your way, among the signs of whatever may be described as event, back to what may be described as presence.) Take a glance at the *Vérmező*, the Field of Blood. And The Bastion above it. Consider the calm of the wounded, who are used to it. Observe them (in the relationship they used to exist in too), then—even more clearly—take proper account of the curve, as the archaeological dig arranges itself at the foot of the hill. So. Now the picture is focused.

You do, of course, remember when they finished it? Were you there, at the end? Were you also at the opening? It has broadened since then. It is competitive. The escalator wells were not quite . . . never mind. Track control. Construction company. Junction point.

You do of course remember the lemon-yellow rubbers? The food packages of the world? The terrain between certainty and uncertainty? You do remember the *Vérmező*, don't you? The archaeological dig at the foot of the hill? The relationships that once existed? The transformation? The construction company? The airport? You do remember the town?

You were there at the opening, weren't you?

Translated by George Szirtes

WHEN SHE LOOKED BACK . . .

When she looked back her face had disappeared.
When she looked back.
The masks that she inhabited
dissolved in earth; green, blue and black
in smeary piles of brow and head
the very last time she looked back.

As soon as she had turned away
two wings, her wings,
began to glow beneath the ray,
the purest silver, wings and lungs
which slowly opened as to fly
an inch or so, then closed again
as she breathed out.

I saw it all,
I saw then they belonged, to me,
not others, sadly, but to me:
between my shoulder blades she flew
like something light had shivered through,
no mask to stunt her backward view.

Translated by George Szirtes

ZSUZSA BENEY

(1930–2006)

FAREWELL

For they are the closest, those who never lived,
like a water-beaded well which I have forgotten,
memory ripens in its bone-shelled kernel
onto forgetting.

I, who exploded in the severe sky
on star-built cart, now that I look back:
behind me, mossy gloaming faintly illuminates—
within me is the lamp,

within me, the path.—You, my cart-trampled being,
wandering pathless below in the mud,
you whose countenance gleams in the moonlight—
hide your face in the stone, the shrubs.

Translated by Ottilie Mulzet

LAKE

Across sweeping lands wreathed in gold
light mist arises; it diffuses, spreads,
tree-lined alleys spin; in the distance lies the vista
of green shadows dispersed by groves.

Like glass within its own illumination
transparency's crystalline realm
its layers enclosing into the horizon
the water's surface, plucked by sun and moon.

But the shore willows, growing asunder,
shudder as the doubled crowns
of the trees tear through

vanishing light-membranes—as below in the lakebed
the vortex of the sky swirls darkly:
opening are the channels of the soul.

Translated by Ottilie Mulzet

ORPHEUS AND EURYDICE (1989) (SELECTIONS)

They say I've become old and sad,
my hair gone grey, my figure dried out.
I no longer see myself.

My gaze is only in his gaze now.
A bridge of light above the white evening.

They say: my tulle winding sheet became a veil of fog,
My bridal dress my shroud.

I no longer see myself.
Nor do I see him whom I followed like a blind shadow
in the semi-darkness infiltrating the street.

*

I see no one, no one else apart from him.
And yet: on the periphery of my vision,
an accumulation of cars, horses, mountains,

transmuted cities: forms never before glimpsed.
Familiar break of day: existence.

Already I do not recognize the world's
one-time shape. With butterfly eyes, oblivion

fell upon it, scattering its pollen.
I don't know how I recognized you.
Like brook water streaming down a cliff.

*

The world is more beautiful, now that I returned
among its lights from shadowlessness.
Although I left my shadow with you.

You were my shadow. I live, shadowless,
the one free creature in the daylight.

*

Perhaps it was not for you that I went among
the shades. To follow, step by step,
your night-black shadow within myself.

Only I glimpsed your frail beauty
in the silver scales of your dying.

Upon my body, the death-sweat froze.
And meanwhile, you, from desire, from pain,

Upon your lute, you wove my shroud lace.
Still, horrified, you saw my arrival
as you called: let there be someone for you to lament.

*

And then I could not break away
from the second death that awaited you.
The first pain had been fulfilled

but the second promised miracles
unseen by the living, not sensed by the dead.

As from stone, there slowly forms
the brilliance of a face not from stone

My soul awakened to your voice.
The weight of your gaze lifted me
from my death onto a more radiant death.

*

I awoke, but then still dreamt.
I saw you, but only in outline.

I knew you were my husband, but only that
moment lived with ever greater illumination
when in your arms I plunged into dream.

*

And I will be there in the not-remembering.
Because whoever has eaten the fruits of these

Crowned trees below the ground, who has drunk
of this spring that has never seen light—
in their eyes, no picture is reflected.

Translated by Ottilie Mulzet

FUGUE

To eat grapes in bed, in January.
To stitch and sew what is not needed.
To bid farewell in the melting darkness.
To be reborn as we say goodbye.

To stifle the fever of new beginnings.
To clean, before travelling.
To not believe in God. To live with God.
To hope. To renounce everything.

To not fear death, solitude.
To not be with others. To not break off.
To touch each other with the beam
of a gaze. To remember. To remain.

Translated by Ottilie Mulzet

TATTERED DETAILS I

We have grown old. But beneath your skin,
your ribs, like ocean waves,
in my naked palm.

Fidgeting among stones in weed-memories
into gypsum beds, into coffins:
tattered details.

That which has changed, has sunk.
The moths have flown away.
Emptiness with its detritus-weight.

An opening window glints, brown-crimson
twilight, then crumbling stairs of brick.
Why exactly these?

All along, the ever-renewing eddies
of times of day, the wooden merry-go-round, its
hopeless yearning.

Above a grey river, metallic sky.
The dead who awaken me every day.
The self of another land.

That black point, the plunging
upwards, the beating of the rain
of forgetting.

Darkness splashing into the room.
Nocturnal suffocation. The glazed shimmering
of dawn.

The message? Paralysed vocal cords, the word
thrashes around in the dust. Birds
without air.

Translated by Ottilie Mulzet

TATTERED DETAILS II

The fog billowed in through the door with us.
Beyond the tiny window, its paint peeling off,
darkness. Inside, blinking, was home.

*

Pain, which sometimes cleaves
through the body like muscle groups loosening:
memory of love.

*

The ancient world, growing dark like coal,
the ever deeper, harder pavement,
the winter night grown chilled like death.

*

Only enough strength to weep
for them surrounding my catafalque:
Now they step back into darkness.

Translated by Ottilie Mulzet

TATTERED DETAILS III

I can bring you back from the earth,
from the underworld—but not even the strength of God
can bring you back from the smoke.

I remember the house, the plate glass windows.
Now I only see yellow walls, and in the walls,
absences.

Now there is no time for me to sweep up.
In the place of furniture, in the corners, on the floor,
are tattered details.

Not one—my love broken to shards.
Water leaks out of a cracked glass.
From dust we came, to dust we return.

No coffin, burial, no grave is needed
for my death to be received. The body
disintegrates within itself.

The face of Fayum, the eyes, eyebrows,
A mirror reflecting the void.
Beauty without object.

Perhaps there will be someone who will see
my face. Behind the mask of the skull,
light-shadows' reflecting flames.

Winter. A glass hemisphere covers the sky.
It cracks, snow pours in through
the crevices; between the snowflakes is the void.

Spring, summer, fragrances long ago floated away
and colours: all radiating from within.
The rose is dying on my mother's dress.

Autumn. The scent of dead leaves, quince and earth
penetrating through the walls. My collapsing
last love.

Translated by Ottilie Mulzet

ORPHEUS AND EURYDICE (2003) (SELECTIONS)

'Our grove has withered,' the trees rustling
within us, birds, morning, and twilight.
God is dying within us.

Accept creation from the one
you have created. Allow the non-created
nothing-wind to traverse your bones.

*

As water splashing in the depths
of wells, we dip our buckets in
the evenings of our childhood.

No trace remains of living material.
the soul mixes into the air.
Falling-star love flickers out.

*

Memory vanishes, there only remains
a crimson light reflected on the window.
Not existence, but its mirror image.

The wound of the last word, broken off,
bleeds for a long time. It is overgrown by final silence
only slowly.

*

The rose, then its wilted stalk, then
its memory, then not even that. The infinite
cathedral of existence is oblivion.

Translated by Ottilie Mulzet

THE RIVER

Through what sluices has it swept
before it finally reached my home
of clay soil and carved its crumbling bed?
Eternity humming from its dark source.

The non-transparent water shows time
only its wrinkled silk surface.
Mirror images of sparkling light.
Waves sliding one under the other.

Broken tiles in the mirror,
cracking, and still another glass,
between was and will be, I became / I'll not be,
running water's burning catharsis.

Translated by George Szirtes

DUST

There's nothing I hate more than dust
in corners of the room, in understanding.
But I can no longer clean everything.
I've strength enough for work, but not for cleanness.

I live in half-light. Literally half-light.
My eyes no longer tolerate the sun.
My heart can't manage all your empathies.
I don't look into death's eyes unafraid.

Because there are no gates of death, just slow
gatherings of dust. Mud and dirt cover our lives.
They gather in the corners of our souls.
We can't step into the light for fear of drowning.

Translated by George Szirtes

I STAND . . .

I stand in the open door, cold flooding
in, coarse night, for years we believed
this was the last autumn evening.
The last farewell.

The wind lifts fog and cloud barriers
up towards the stars. It is dark,
white and grey and fog-dark.
Like souls on the old paintings,

everything that is moves, turns, eddies.
God, if you are there, why is no light cast?
God, if you existed, you wouldn't leave me here by myself
on this first winter evening.

Translated by Ottilie Mulzet

INTO THE SPIDERWEB . . .

God, who became entangled
in the spiderweb, woven into our frail,
gleaming thought-filaments,
pupates into a motionless larva.

His trembling wings break off,
the phosphorus lights reflecting
themselves. Our twilight sinks into darkness,
into the hollows of despair.

Liberate yourself, if only for a minute,
break free of us, only for a moment—
lead us across the gates of our deaths
to the further plains of existence, unknown.

Translated by Ottilie Mulzet

THE GUEST

Sleeping on my pillow, never to be disturbed,
like a cat kneading my legs
every night. Already a tangible body, graspable.
I embrace this body, in despair,

like a lover who no longer desires,
compelled precisely by lack of desire, by solitude
to cling to the other. I don't know
what I fear more—disappearance,

or this presence alongside me to the end of time.
Before I knew him, I walked through woods,
through fields, I glided like the wind,
I escaped like Kore in her disguise.

Translated by Ottilie Mulzet

THE TREE

Every year it dies, then it is born,
its existence does not cease in winter.
Yet it is mortal: its crown of branches
shall one day be torn asunder by that wind

which is nowhere. Its trunk will be cleaved open
by a lightning bolt slumbering within time.
Just as its cessation within existence,
just as, within, the throbbing

of winter and spring. Like its consciousness of itself
in the fullness of silence. More than the rustling
of leaves, falling across the web of words.
Not a creation rooted in time.

Translated by Ottilie Mulzet

SILENCE

1

This silence is not the infinity
of childhood, when gripped by spasms,
you almost suffocated, before the sluice gates
of weeping crashed open,

it is not the leaf-whispering of years gone by
which, if mute for a single moment,
rattled us awake; an awakening, perhaps,
that chilled the world unto death.

Nor is it the dread that lay within dark, ancient material.
Nor the beating of the heart, constrained.
It is mute weight, felt for the first time
amid the depths of things.

2

This silence is not the self-extinguishing
interference of the clear sounds of metal tubes
being struck, nor is it the snags of curves
sinking into the void, intersecting each other,

neither is it the deep shuddering of material
and spirit traversing one another,
nor is it the tamped-down breath
of ascending devotion, nor is it the screech

of the air ripped apart
like silk. This silence is the chaos
of sounds torn away from existence,
when existence no longer hears itself.

Translated by Ottilie Mulzet

THE TRANSLATOR

He steps into the poem. Rock. It closes
behind him, he too becomes rock.
He becomes absorbed in the cell
of the bones, in their vaulted arcades.

But while he freezes, the clay about him
roasts at white heat, eventually melts,
and from the glowing magma there blossoms
a whole new framework, the rose in the desert.

And as for him, he turns from rock, is enclosed
within the rock, is resurrected, vanishes
on the road that leads through his body
from fullness into wholeness.

Translated by George Szirtes

NOVEMBER 1956

Autumn shot through with bullets. In place of
the heart, the leaves' absence
shows through.

*

Their edges did not spin together.
The wound: timeless
time between dying and death.

*

One season on a leaf. Shroud.
The shadow of green silk or
absence white as snow.

*

It died before
it could have fallen. Would it had lived
without the fatal bullet?

Translated by Ottilie Mulzet

THE MUTE WORD

In the deluge of sounds, three words without sound—
Let there be—hover between what is above and below.
The rubble of three words holds
the disintegrating world horizontally,

a world which no longer gives birth—it only passes.
The clattering veneer of things
covers the silence deep within.
The thread-frail music of existence.

And yet no sudden gust arises, no raging blaze,
not the storm's lilac lights,
but a soft, gentle voice: Elijah
permeates the karst walls of our burial chamber.

Translated by Ottilie Mulzet

ÁGNES GERGELY

(1933–)

MIDNIGHT BURIAL

Saint David has gone mad.
Somewhere a grave is dug.
For the slovenly procession
the violin, moans, weeps, sobs.

Slowly the snow is falling,
or dandelions keep raining down—
a lamp's square light on the road,
perhaps dawn will never come.

Meandering through the dark,
a choral society, in black,
alleyways taper off, they step
into the moonlight replete.

Humming sacred Latin words,
the procession walks along.
On the crooked roof
sits a shepherd's-crook-tailed cat.

Candlesticks overturned:
the monks' hoods hover.
On the hilltops, people
shut their windows closed.

In the gorge sits a bird.
Is silent, deep in tangled grove.
In between the shutters
someone rattles a violin bow.

Who is strong, this evening
shall no longer awaken.
The bird's feather will shiver
with the temples of his dreams.

Translated by Ottilie Mulzet

I LOOKED INTO THE WELL

I looked into the well, and nothing did I see:
I knew long ago—nothing in its depths.
A madman once jumped into its water,
even then, in the well there was no air.

And yet still, how vertiginous the edge
beyond desire, before danger's advent.
Below, the green-edged moon-sliver trembles,
flies and spiders swing on it to and fro.

You stay here though you feel afraid,
splashing sounds as if rising from below;
holding on tight above the abyss,
while furtively you lean down low, low, low.

Translated by Ottilie Mulzet

SMALL TOWN

The moon became a cobalt hatchet,
the sky a blue-slatted fence,
between them swung the town hall's tower—
we strolled.

Below, the square was splinters of fine silver
the Holy Trinity askew, its harrowed Baroque
angels—the tepid grass, blaring like the beating
of wings.

And I waited for the birds atop the linden trees
to commence their sharp shrieking,
to awaken, from its intoxicating dreams, the colossal
doll-city.

The bells tolled. Above, on the electrical wires,
immeasurable sparks were sundered apart
with a complicit message, calling at midnight
somewhere.

And from the lake, across the lilac park,
through the beaten alleyways between the grates,
there came floating, like weightless clumps of earth, the frogs'
heartbeats.

My eardrums deceived me—the path was only this much.
In the lock, a key clattered far away.
I walked there, I marched beside you
on stork's legs.

Translated by Ottilie Mulzet

YOU ARE A SIGN ON MY DOOR POST

To my dead father

I have no memories,
and even if I do, I don't hang onto them.
I never yearned for cemeteries,
and organic chemistry doesn't bother me.

But sometimes around the month of November,
if it's foggy, and behind the damp windows
I'm struggling for air
without even being able to see your form
—knowing nothing of the whereabouts of your body—
one of your movements trickles upward.

I sense, between your long, nervous fingers
a thermos turning around, a blunt can opener,
a pocket knife, a backpack opened wide,
warm undergarments, a prayer book,
and your back, beneath this weightless burden,
cracks and realizes: it can bear the weight.
I sense you setting out. You step out, well-dressed wanderer,
you never depart, you only set out,
laughing, you look back, thirty-eight years old,
I'll be home soon, you nod, you point,

—the next day would have been your birthday—
and whimpering, you weep inside, like a painting by Mednyánszky,
and you wave—how you are waving!

You are a sign on my door post: you are stuck there;
The Ferdinánd Bridge, the palm-sized grate,
the sludge-filled path, the final weakening, the devouring of grass
are all just blind imaginings, the mind's inventions,
for surely I was lying, I used to see you
beneath the suffocating November sky,
you set off with me, you breathe, your tears
squeeze my throat, and I leave them there,
and up above, where it should not be
that thin Memphis cigarette knocked out of your mouth
burns through the skin on a star.

Translated by Ottilie Mulzet

BITTER ROOT

Root, root, little root,
little veins flesh-coloured,
where're you from, loamy one,
you newcomer that toils?

What fate grew up with you
above, below the ground,
with your leaves that shudder,
oh bitter, bitter root?

What giant
millennial layers
nursed you all these years?
What are the memories
of hailstones and downpours
that you still preserve?

What kind of sun shone down,
how oft did the hoe strike,
did minerals starve you,
did a whirlwind set you down?

How come you weren't ripped out?
What sustained you,
your leaves stretching out,
oh bitter, bitter root,

show me your fingers,
cover up your depths,
little frantic being
who grasps so hard at life.

No matter what wind brought you
nor how oft it stands in wait
you shall never leave here,
oh bitter, bitter root.
Here is where you must feel
the simoom in your waist.
Here is where you must grow.
Here—where you must decay.

Translated by Ottilie Mulzet

UNDER A PANNONIAN SKY

By the wine-press house, the road turns off
to the right, I see low village roofs

through the mountains, on roads burnished blue,
I'm a stranger here, for I intrude

no one in sight, only acacias, vineyards
sand-built houses beneath antennas

between wine cellars, under the Pannonian sky
a small donkey—grey prophet—walks by

waves back with ears of mother-of-pearl
respectable plebians once lived here

five hundred years ago, the wandering carts
of merchants left their traces in these parts

and here, watching time in its fury,
were gentle bakers making bread from honey

from the castle came sounds of music, dance,
with its Italian lights, the Renaissance

wherever their handcart travelled, passing by
a road grew longer under the Pannonian sky

and perhaps, donning his brown kaftan
my ancestor also tread this path

he stood, as I do now, next to the road,
looked round, was fearful, uttered pious words

and here, more practical, was yet another,
sewing boots of fine Moroccan leather

my great-great grandmother, small, amber-eyed
keeping a watch on all the stray dogs

she sent the children to play outside,
went out to gather herbs and she sang

the psalms, the tanning smell floating everywhere,
between the hills, the edges of the fields

struggling with biting wind, winter storms
resurrected from the stomachs of worms

on they went, their footprints trailing silver
pretty like drifting smoke, uninvited

just as I hew to this clump of earth of mine
they were protected by the Pannonian sky

the road looms blue from here to beyond
flee this place—run away, whoever can.

Translated by Ottilie Mulzet

INTERPRETATION OF DREAMS

The dust incandescent on the prison wall.
'So tell us, Joseph, since you are the seer . . .'
The stone on fire, the earth, crockery of squalor.
The cup-bearer, the baker stood trembling.

Joseph looked at the prison bars; he spoke to them,
gently: 'Three times the sun shall turn.
The Lord will save the life of one of you—
the other will be devoured by birds.'

Did he know what he was saying? And whence
the intimation of this infallible fever?
Did he know—silence too was an answer?

But he spoke. The one sent to live—lived,
the one sentenced to death—a corpse.
From the apparition, none may ever hide.

Translated by Ottilie Mulzet

SIGNAL LIGHTS

That strange body, standing close to me,
took hold of my arm,
the oblique rail-line in my head
said—the train was approaching.

Chilled to the bones by this knowledge,
Nothing now that can protect.
The bodies and hours are leaving,
The darkness turns to signs.

Translated by Ottilie Mulzet

CHURCH TOWER

It's as if the two church towers
could collapse on me.
My neck caught between its two gables,
its insignia
would puncture my eyebrows,
my hip bones knocked
against the prayer house's marble ship.
With iron-tipped arms, plunging backward,
signalling its enormous solitude to the sky,
a cat walks on glass, meowing for bread.
I am saved.

Translated by Ottilie Mulzet

FISHES

I never understood them:
fleeing from water, jumping.

If it's more natural with gills,
then why this other milieu—suffocating—

the gaseous, the ungraspable,
during collisions, unsplashable,

for what reason? Why?
To show off their scales' shine.

In the Great Waterwheel, to stop, for a moment.
In the sky, to stop, for a moment.

Then law begins to function.
The sky sinks down—gravitation,

the unreachable takes form,
swings in the place that is known,

enormous drop of water, heaven enforced,
Hungary, my hopeless love.

Translated by Ottilie Mulzet

ON THE NATURE OF LIGHT

for Judit Márványi

A butterfly on the balcony;
outside, an angel in the garden.
Who carries a lantern in lieu of a body,
untouchable.
One of the flutterings is like the sky.
The other, enclosed in time.
Bearing death, who stands among them.
Only it emits light.

Translated by Ottilie Mulzet

PRAYER BEFORE LIGHTS OUT

Lord, save me from perfection
like the wedge-shaped burn marks on the edge
of the ironing blanket: leave upon me
my mistakes, the trace of your hand. In this city,
where the two shores watch each other grimacing,
draw upon me a Dutch tulip field. And if you write
upon your objects: 'warning, high-voltage',
place me as an accomplice in your electrical circuit. The
evening star can be seen so infrequently, guardian
of the sheep flocks of old. Among the cumulus clouds, in
this world forced apart, we do not see each other.
In my singed, ruinous, short-circuited bones
with their memories of ancient beings,
let me emit light, while darkness falls.

Translated by Ottilie Mulzet

CEMETERY IN PANNONIA

Lovely and narrow, so many stones
 beneath the cypress trees—
Should you ask about the name—it's
 6 Kozma Street.

If your aching heart needs rest
 as the sorrowful doves here meet,
awaiting you with opened arms is
 6 Kozma Street.

Large are the gardens of Rakoskeresztúr,
 Kerepes and Farkasrét—
but how small dear and intimate a place is
 6 Kozma Street.

The Catholic Cemetery
 any Catholic will take—
but we don't know who's buried at
 6 Kozma Street.

If you are Lutheran or Baptist
 or Calvinist in belief—
not indicated by address is
 6 Kozma Street.

O Lord, how I do favour
symbols of all categories—
but what is emblemized by
6 Kozma Street?

Will the anti-Kozma forces
finally concede defeat
if placed in parentheses is
(6 Kozma Street)?

Life is merely sign language—
and death more inclined to sleep,
but all graves are dug the same at
6 Kozma Street.

Beneath the Pannonian sky
let not propriety be displeased—
For what kind of information is
6 Kozma Street!

The mere statistic of your being
represents no increase.
Here you lived—even more dead than
6 Kozma Street.

Translated by Ottilie Mulzet

COSMOPOLITAN

Because death can pounce on you anywhere.
The deceitful love the cloak
of foreignness. Then a familiar light will fall
upon your lost steps. Perhaps
even your mother tongue will not prove
any kind of handhold. Hades will be more
than even your country was at one time.
What is needed is the darkness of mythology,
so you can encounter the incomprehensible
fog-thicket of whom you believe
that beyond the grave, like in a ballad, you can nestle
close together, two flower stalks.
But the cries for help of wickedness,
stubborn dictates will be enfolded
into prayers, the roaring of the sea. Romeo's ladder
hangs there above the charred
depths. You offer oblivion,
the task of the Other,
to the pursuers. Yet the mistaken and their delusions
will be charred as one. Look at your wound.
The genuine wound. Always at the wound.
You can build your temple anywhere.

Translated by Ottilie Mulzet

SHOOTING IN TERÉZVÁROS

Those deep entranceways.
So many flowers can fit in that ditch, you say.
So many screams, I answer.
The call for help ricocheting from wall to wall.
All around, the city is silent.
At the base of the stone cross, no one steals by,
wrapping a flowing cape around himself.
Soon it will be dark.
The bouquet turned to straw clatters onto the stone pedestal.
The bell is tolling—it tolls for someone else here.
The execution is now over.

Translated by Ottilie Mulzet

PSALM 137

We sat by the rivers of Babylon.
We wept. Babylon is without a sea.
Our harp is on the willow. Torment speaks with a different voice.
Sweat is needed from us, not passion.
And not principles—for why has the blood flowed from our veins.
May Amen be inscribed on my right arm grown cold,
if I forget you, Jerusalem.

The people claw our sign into the wall.
Who incites them—for they know not what they do.
A royal sign, it has outlived many other signs.
Do not blame them, my Lord, their transgression!
Do not thrown their beautiful infants to the wall . . . !
May my face, its suffering, be convulsed onto my mouth,
If I forget you, János Arany.

Translated by Ottilie Mulzet

BARCAROLE

The decade is slowly foundering now
desire drifts on a raft beneath the house
the towers are playing Monteverdi
a yellow moon spreads across the canal

the yellow moon, trembling yellow blotch
a single bell rope hangs within the tower
the raft incandescent like the inside of a lamp
a colossal lamp, the continent

the continent is slowly sinking now
raft tower canal and Gulag
Petrograd, three heart attacks, a paper mill
yellow moon spreading on the psych ward

the yellow blotch, the yellow blotch trembling
well-wall-sized existence in the canal
grants water city for water city
while Akhmatova slowly looks down

Translated by Ottilie Mulzet

FROM THE YEARS OF BARBARISM

Golyev, sergeant-at-arms, killed First Lieutenant
Ilyin during the duel. Next, the sergeant
blasted apart the city's more important buildings,
among them the eighteenth-century Byelchev Palace,
along with its stucco ornaments and
Baroque stables.

I report, Your Majesty,
the stucco ornaments were superfluous. What is the point
of dazzling the barbarians? The city is sustained
by its proportions; the tensile force of destruction.
What you are soaring across is not a chasm.
The only measurement is plunging. On the mountain peaks,
the horseman is only a horseman when they catch up with him;
otherwise he is the statue of a horseman.

Do you hear, Your Majesty?
The bells are tolling for First Lieutenant Ilyin.
I recall when he sat before me in the Academy,
his fists always sweating during weaponry class.
Now he can perspire, even for eternity. Here
history is measured with my own steps.
'He who killed him.' 'He who fired the shots.'
Steps into legend. And the depths of time—
wait a moment, Your Majesty—

like landslides
shifting lava, make both our syntheses gape open wide.
'He did not die because of him, but instead of him.'

Translated by Ottilie Mulzet

CHARADE

1

As in the forest, I trip on a branch,
enigma in the tree, horror.
Chanting, selling rose bouquets,
a beggar woman. The vagrant crowd

moving between fried-bread sellers.
Do not be easy, if God strikes.
Your body bleeds like heavy light
onto the temple, 'away, away from here',

the labyrinths are echoing.
From here? Where? Why? With whom?
Only because the thorns whisper
feral letters with their dead tongues?!

The bells are begging, the people deaf.
The apse, the floor, awash with blood.
To get back to the cupola,
I stagger and speak no words.

2

I stagger and speak no words.
to get back to the cupola.
The apse, the floor awash with blood.
The bells are begging, the people deaf.

feral letters with their dead tongues
only because the thorn whispers—
From here? Where? Why? With whom?
The labyrinths are echoing

your body bleeds through, 'away, away from here',
onto the temple like heavy light.
Do not be easy, if God strikes.
Moving between fried-bread sellers,

a beggar woman. The vagrant crowd
chanting, selling rose bouquets,
enigma in the tree, horror.
As in the forest, I trip on a branch.

3

Enigma in the tree, horror
your body bleeds through, 'away, away from here',
feral letters with their dead tongues
to get back to the cupola—
do not be easy, if God strikes.

Translated by Ottilie Mulzet

HE COMES THIS WAY AFTER FIVE IN THE AFTERNOON

He comes this way after five in the afternoons.
Always on foot.
Wearing his cloak and wide-brimmed hat.
Wearing boots, maybe heavy ones.
Around his feet, the invisible
children's choir blares.
All the while, in the ship's hold
hell has broken loose.

Blame yourself, if he comes by this way.
Yourself, not someone else, only yourself.
Do not point up at the stars.
Point to the dust. Down into the dust.
Nevermore up to the stars.
Always to the dust.

Translated by Ottilie Mulzet

TO MIKLÓS ZRÍNYI

What should I do with the fortress of Sziget,
Drégely or Eger—what are they to me?
To the estimable raising of the flag
I was never summoned.

What should I do with ancient Buda Castle—
guard its lock, its yataghan?
When the Sultan took over the key
I was not at hand.

What am I to do with Mohács,
with its empty-running brooks?
I stood in the Austrian death camps
beneath the mute shower taps.

What should I do with this sentence:
'To the Hungarian, do no harm!'
Everyone I ever loved
always perished in the end.

Translated by Ottilie Mulzet*

*NOTES

the fortress of Sziget: fortifications built in 1420; *Drégely or Eger*: Drégely is the site of fortifications built in the 13th century; Eger is home to a castle that experienced both Mongol and Ottoman invasions; *yataghan*: Ottoman sword; *Mohács*: the site of the definitive Hungarian defeat by Ottoman troops in 1526; *'To the Hungarian, do no harm!'* (*„Ne bantsd a Magyart!"*): In 1661, Count Miklós Zrínyi wrote a tract entitled *Medicament against Turkish Opium*, castigating his fellow Hungarians for not sufficiently resisting Ottoman rule. It was reissued in 1790 under the title *To the Hungarian, do no harm!* The phrase become a rallying cry for Hungarian nationalism and independence.

HOUSE AT VILLAGE'S END

At half past five, they look up at the moon,
then they look through the Book.
At half past six the candle is used up—
it's when the miracles come round.

At that time, they go from house to house,
So many of them unknown.
They are not wearing black hoods.
Outside the slant fog drizzles down.

No harp is playing, no violin,
they bring no frozen prophecy.
But the one who understands them best
has lurked around cemeteries.

In the harmonic theory
of stones they reside,
after five nights' passing renewed:
the moon-halo of the dead.

All who live there converge,
entangled on the parchment.
Pale tallow-women dancers hang
on the silver candelabrum.

Translated by Ottilie Mulzet

PILGRIMS

Few are the meadow's signposts.
Few are the light signals.
Few the immediate faces.
Few, as well, the angels.

That rustling—only butterfly wings.
The ocean still far away.
Few are the windmills, the wind.
The sky holds its narrow tent.

My pain, all clamped together
tries to walk on here.
And must move on, must keep stepping,
as it goes bereft of words.

Unaccustomed to silence
is the crowd, frightened.
Few are the hands, the muteness,
the buildings that are silent.

This is mirage or summons,
the oak forest is grumbling.
The light of the chiselled stars
obsessively is dying.

Few are the meadow's signposts.
Hardly a crumb of bread.
May the rustling sounds
last till tomorrow at dawn.

Translated by Ottilie Mulzet

INCONNU

The crooked street darkens
the city's diseased lungs.
Drags to its entrance gates
the one unafraid of the heavens.

The stars' great dream, lashing,
like the oracle signs of old.
Compass, mast, mizzen-sail:
the captain hovers there as well.

Where the shadows dart upwards,
mercy, burnt to its stump
reaps along the shore—
when the moon begins to sink,

the city, diseased, grows darker,
no nearby angel, no miracle,
the waves beat at the shore,
no matter who sent them there,

for everything recoils away,
Inconnu, the semi-darkness speaks,
memory excised from body and soul,
memoir, diagnosis—subtracted,

if having stepped to prayer, to the bridge,
the crossing will never be made.
Mercy burnt down to its stump,
Inconnu, the trumpet sounds.

Translated by Ottilie Mulzet

INHERITANCE

They walked here once. From their steps
nothing is built, only words.
Build no monument to them.
For every work can be tarnished.

But memory will preserve itself.
From the scar, there will grow a stump.
Unseemly proximity to death
can be inherited, like time.

Where you arise, ask the river,
only do not ask why it arose.
As Seneca always taught:
your life is in your own hands.

Translated by Ottilie Mulzet

GIZELLA HERVAY

(1934–82)

ONE PAIN

is like the next
wearing even
the Sundays thin

I live underground
the soul goes limp

my beloved children
standing always at the ready
proxy death

a plane comes—I panic
and flee in word-hurricane

my son: child shirt dream
I walk your ways

think of me under the ground
of your eyes only the sky remains

my little lead soldier
death has knocked you flat on your back

my son my son
my death my life

Translated by Erika Mihálycsa

A BEGINNER AT DEATH AMONG YOU

with hole-pierced forehead
bared hands
I step backward among you
my coat in the wind turned
inside out

balancing with umbrella
on time's tautened rope
bowing over the fallen
with orphan hope

bread and knife they seized
departing on luxury trains
we stay behind with our bare bones
eternal earthdwellers

Translated by Erika Mihálycsa

THE PETRIFIED MOTHER

holds her dead son
in her lap

carries him away across
foreheads

puts him down by the shores
of mouths

delivers
death
anew

Translated by Erika Mihálycsa

STANDING ALONE

in the cut-down forest

exiled
on uninhabited planet

they forbade the plural
in dog-cold loneliness

mud-fallen foreheads
wiped-out memories

in homeless homeland

Translated by Erika Mihálycsa

THIS CELL

that I've measured for myself
is my homeland

bells
within barrage of gunfire
the cannonball hits me

above my head
the epitaph
finds its way home

Translated by Erika Mihálycsa

BLOOD DRIES

on the face of the earth

worries
tear up the trees from the root

nights squat
under pimpled sky

in shop windows
smashed-in brows

skulls studded
with stones

revelation
attached to bread

on the third day
bones under the sand

Translated by Erika Mihálycsa

GRACE VISITS ME

prisonguard death
grace visits me

I've applied for a homeland
they granted me an extension
measured in rationed bread

on Mondays and Fridays
a glass of water
on Mondays and Fridays

flowers on Sunday
loveless
bed aslant

my son on a picture
seal of my under-
ground life on my mouth

Translated by Erika Mihálycsa

BECAUSE OUR SUFFOCATION IS SENSATIONAL

and our poems like the day's gossip
are taken from one metropolis to the next
we burrow deep into the earth, we bloom
into earth-clots bleached to bone
but won't put bilge into the mouths
of morticians with plastic wreaths
the soul of bells is no divine grace
no reams of garters hanging down
our head is the globe itself
and our seas no salivating place
for amphibian luxury tourists
dignified we pace up and down behind
bars if necessary we yell and swear
but won't auction off the world we won't
bargain with leather jackets
we won't spit into flower cups
won't rat out our dead to them

Translated by Erika Mihálycsa

I'LL NAIL YOU TO MY LOINS

speak with me not with endingness
I'll give birth to you anew just to see you
I'll wrench your mouth your eyes one by one from winter
reconquer for summer the odour of your clothes
from winter claim back the snow of your skin
wrap up your shivering words
I'll stand upright in hissing wind, your flag

Translated by Erika Mihálycsa

I COME WITH FUSILLADE WITH LOVE

the sunflower goes up in flames
milkweed bares its milk teeth
dung-flies alight upon your eye
snowfalls tripping backward, they fall
roe deer hang on butchers' hooks
woe your helmet is full of blood
woe my helmet is full of blood

Translated by Erika Mihálycsa

FOR YOU I WILL KNEEL

confess to every single war
including the real war growing
behind my ribs and now I'm
horrified of everything
flesh falls off my face
the woods fall from my loins
the raspberries from my breasts
my bulging belly bursts open
lo I'm a potato sack, my Lord

blackbird on your finger

Translated by Erika Mihálycsa

LODEN COAT ON THE HOOK OF EASTERN EUROPE

we put it on in turn
in the common rain
waste falls from our mouth
rusty nails from our hair
plaster from our faces
above our heads an interchangeable
loden coat in the sky
maps of interchangeable destinies
interchangeable deaths
brass buttons of interchangeable faiths
bowels of interchangeable peoples
lipstick stains of interchangeable loves
interchangeable hooks interchangeable
loden coats hanging in the wind

Translated by Erika Mihálycsa

I WRITE LIKE ONE SENTENCED TO DEATH

writing a letter home
each poem has an addressee
but I won't rat out their names
hoping to remain as name-
less as the rest of you
namelessly fallen wretched
hoping you will
countersign my eyes, nameless ones

Translated by Erika Mihálycsa

FROM YOUR WOMB HOMELAND YOU EXPELLED ME

From your womb homeland you expelled me
they hold me up from my feet
yell—they slap me
my mother's lap is full of blood

they stick a number to my arm
they weigh me
I puke milk
blood gushes from my mother's breast

Translated by Erika Mihálycsa

SUPERIOR PINK TOILET SOAP

superior pink toilet soap
on the coal heaver's pink bathtub
his daughters in white pleated skirts
in state sanatorium
a five-lei bill on the desk
in superior housing blocks
on an inferior village's edge
five lei in the schoolmistress' hand
on a superior lorry
inferior unqualified workers
in their inferior village sacks
loaves of superior city bread
inferior five-lei lives
in superior rhythmic clapping
in lipstick stuttering
drafted into the army naked

Translated by Erika Mihálycsa

FREE FALL. ORATORIO FOR THREE VOICES (SELECTIONS)

It's as if you could hear,
as if I still loved you.
(Paul Celan)

Another storey of loneliness.
In your breathing I sleep in.

Another storey of loneliness.
My breathing harshes against your mouth's edge.
Another storey of loneliness.
You sit out above me on the sky.
Another storey of loneliness.
I freefall into your palm.
My clotted hair
trickles down your face.
Another storey of loneliness.
This morning I killed myself
and landed here, alive . . .
Another storey of loneliness.
. . . where there is no I, no you,
only us
no past, no future, only presence.

Another storey of loneliness.
In your palm the hills are born anew,
in your wrinkles the roads converge
where I've been, where I'm bound to.
Another storey of loneliness.
The cloud rises,
I lie under your
eyes in the grass.
Another storey of loneliness.
Yet again the sun, from brow to brow . . .
Another storey of loneliness.
. . . rises and sets
until we glimpse each other.
Another storey of loneliness.
It is dawn. I am the sun.
One sentence
we write in two
that you couldn't without me
that I couldn't without you.
This tree now speaks with its leaves.
If I can't answer it loses heart
and retreats among its fellow trees.
There is no aloneness
only our fear
from the encounter.
Another storey of loneliness.
Now I'll inscribe the wrinkle in my brow
for you to recognize me
if I lose my way.
Another storey of loneliness.
From my brow the road trickles into nothingness—
if you don't find me
I will forget you.

Another storey of loneliness.
If you don't come soon
I will reorganize your face
retouch you blank.
Another storey of loneliness.
The hollows of the houses in construction
emigrate under the verdant sky.

The echo falls back
into the defenceless throat.
The sky is emptied out.
There's always someone to answer.
Who does this sentence rebound from?
I ask you: someone else answers.
Love ripples off in rings,
every child is of everyone,
every sentence endless.
Time goes round in roundelay,
ever higher, ever lower,
there's always someone to answer.
We move into each other's eyes.
I look at you from so close up
that I lose sight of you.
The sky is emptied out.
This love is not mine
this love is not yours.
There's always someone to answer.
This morning the alarm clock starts
growing—it will never
stop.
We cannot but love like bugs
wriggling for bare survival.
Our faces: mud-sunk landscape,

we can only smile
when trains take us apart.
You are far away
And I live in another absence.
There's always someone to answer.
Call me, write a letter
or send me at least a thread of your hair
so I won't lose my way alone.
Because for three years I believed
you are my right arm
and I, your left.
I have two suns:
your right eye, your left eye.
I wander the earth
under two suns.
Mud-sunk to my elbows
in a tractor track
under the impotent sky,
among dismembered fences
where the thought that doesn't
rebuild the fence is shameful,
in front of the crestfallen houses
where we sit about
to get through tomorrow,
in the well-practiced distrust
where I'm at home—
among black piglets in the dust,
in squatting baby-prattle,
filling a hole with crags,
mud-sunk to my eye whites
with the future's stains
on my brow.
Share the nothing with me
so it becomes something!

I create you anew
from a smile.
One morning we'll start out
with only as much bread
as we can somehow break.
In your smile congealed
on me I stand unmoving.
We sleep in the grass
in hole-elbowed sweaters.
Shame falls, the shirt falls off,
the hourhand falls off the clock.
All the day's messages are ours
but we see only the red and yellow,
can't hear the inarticulate speech of light
but for a flash or two when we love.
But what a horizon line
that we reach our palms into,
high up, to touch the skywinds!
What idiom
that we translate ourselves into,
so the light would understand!
You can't discontinue the waterfall,
the mouth splits, time cascades down.
We put the flowers back in their place.
We furbish the suitcase
to move into
the one shirt
we possess.
I know what comes tomorrow!
The glass of water has a voice.
The bell sequestered behind the ribs
swings beneath the skin—
the future tolling in alarm.

Dawn takes long,
by tomorrow I will forget you.
Dawn takes long,
by tomorrow I will breathe life into you.
We see too much of one another—
we get lost on the body's pathways.
I'm waiting for a signal, for the earth
to open between our words.
Into the same sky we fall.
A shred of sky
in our teeth
exsanguinated hope
and yet every fall
leads upward.
The earth reaches out its hand
with me, to touch its childhood,
but in my arm the movement goes astray
hesitantly
groping
into nothingness.
With the stirring of bombs in our hearts,
anguished before the full plates
we reach out and jerk back
watching the soup steam away.
Would like to reach that hand
concealed by the train . . .
moving into the train . . .
It's in one moment only we can
be at home—
homeless.

***

I'm still dizzy. But before your eyes
I build, alone, a home for myself.
The foetus's smile
glows through my womb.
Agony is getting ready.
Agony is getting ready—
to turn into breath.
Slowly agony turns into breathing
in time's vagitus.
Mary holds the Son in her lap,
In her lap she holds death.
Death looks small in Mary's lap,
in Mary's lap death looks small.
The wrinkled newborn face
of defenceless earth
is the infinite vagitus of birth
in milk dripping down . . .
in the fleeing eye white,
the carapace-less squashable bug
in infinite colliery draught.
Mary is every collier mother.
The foetus's smile glows
through my womb.
I'll give birth to you, one gesture at a time,
your every thread of hair, one by one,
I'll give birth to the world we used to be,
that we'll become, I'll give birth to your death,
I'll give birth to empty space so you be not afraid
if nothing of us is left behind
in infinite exile, only the earth
above: then I'll raise you from the dead.
You sit out above me on the sky.
Who will the upthrown penny hit?

He'll be the catcher.
The catcher is hit by shrapnel
on the temple.
He falls. No pain
just falls.
He who was the catcher
and spared by shrapnel fire,
who stepped out of the burning house's wall
who had to jump on a racing train
will jump on every racing train,
step out of every housewall,
cry last after every countdown,
bet his life on every penny
and hurl it upward into the sky
until it sticks.
Stark raving mad
rattle of trains
our undernourished bodies
run down to smiling
our lean dinner chips of our mugs
our mother's face trickling apart—
I freefall into your eyes
my clotted hair
trickles down your face.
Here I live walled in concrete,
speechless.
My footsoles planted on stone,
my hands are stone.
Can't move my head.
Yet I know how many kinds of sky
cross above,
know it with my hair frozen into concrete,
my fingertips caught between two bricks.

I know the colours of autumn
and night's weight bows down my head.
Morning creeps slowly up my legs
like blood,
I know the earth with my footsoles
as in the times I lived back home.
How many times I died—you know.
I wasted into it. Because I didn't want
to stay alive at all costs.
Because love was no alliance.
Because I didn't want
to stay alive at all costs.
Because love was no alliance.
Sleep tight!
I fall asleep in your breathing.
The flower shaken into the ditch
grows in my womb.
Uncover your skin,
cover yourself in my heartbeat!
I lie in the grass
under your eyes.
At home in freedom.
In unbearable light,
eyes wide open,
beyond the road's end
at the limits of sound
towards your eyes,
towards the source of light.
In the heart of darkness
where it turns to light.
In love's ravines.
On another planet,
another laughter.
Iron bars between the two of us.

On this earth
where I find the way to you.
Thrown here into bomb-crater rifts,
in houses bruised black and blue,
there is no other way but inside the earth:
everything else is covered in barbed wire.
These unending weapons are
raped earth laughing:
—And yet you can't do me in!
I will rise from the dead on the third day!—
idiotic brawling of hope
in front of the sinking houses,
legs are moss grown to the knees,
light crawls upwards from the ground,
shared misery glows
through our transparent palms,
the stable warmth . . .
No death can do in love,
every basin is filled with blood,
our foetuses to nurture.
And tomorrow we will rise again.

Translated by Erika Mihálycsa

MAGDA SZÉKELY

(1936–2007)

THE JUDGEMENT

I may not relent, for I live instead of them
in whom forgiveness may no longer arise.
They do not change—bearing motionless accusation
as earth bears stone.

It is spring. I am eating and I grow.
The quickening flesh stoops towards the living,
I would clutch at the existing world,
like a plant clutching at a stake,

but I must live without mercy,
without forbearance, just as they, the dead.
to remain like a stone upon the earth,
unrelenting in their truth.

The earth heals, their ruptured place
will slowly be filled by the nascent,
their traces by life overgrown.
The last judgement, it is myself.

Translated by Ottilie Mulzet

THE LIVING

It would have been better had I perished with them,
than living like this, so crowded with their deaths.
Swooping down upon me like vultures,
ripping out their parts from within me.

They are right to do so. My body exists instead of theirs.
For sixteen years, I have carried
their final moments. As on the cross,
they hang upon my ambivalent heart.

I would carry them with me further still,
let their weight ferment within me,
let them, like the trees outside,
be ever growing, with renewed strength—

The living grow weak. Perhaps in the end
it is not their final minute I shall carry,
but when, standing on the ditch's edge,
they recalled the taste of a good piece of bread.

Translated by Ottilie Mulzet

PRECIPICE

Whoever ate their Sunday soup
with gusto, or standing calmly on the edge
of the pavement, looking
at the blotch-sized faces
as they stumbled in the procession,
as they were marched, more solitary
than the world's uninhabited regions
towards the wintry Danube banks,

how could they ever know on what cliff,
on the edge of what precipice
with unsteady foothold I stand,
on what barren promontories,
how could they ever know what unwavering force
binds me here, know what it is
that I lift upon my shoulders
alone and lost?

But it is true: I am the one
who lifts them up in my two arms.
And if no one reaches out to me now,
if my muscles should finally give out
if, beneath my feet,

the last drop of humanity should vanish,
if no one should reach out to me,
we shall plunge into the abyss.

Translated by Ottilie Mulzet

SHORE AND SEA

The sea lies in the heavy light
of the sun, and then the moon.
Now clanging, fiery red,
now resting, iron-white.
Every evening was summer,
no downpours ever came,
the glassy water's surface glittered
the sky darkening above it.

We ran along the shore, the two of us
we jumped across the ditches.
The foam swept across our feet,
the dry seaweed grazed against us.
Almost two hours, running
in the wind, down below the camp's
lanterns, its silence. What is left
of the days and nights?

As the vegetation comes undone,
so does every hour within me unfold.
The water pounds my feet,
the spumes erupt and descend.

I run, I run in the currents
of the shore's wind, now alone,
I run, happily, in the wind
towards the lanterns, towards the silence.

Translated by Ottilie Mulzet

THE DAMNED

They leaned over the borders of their being
as far as the mountain peak where I lived.
I saw their pine-tree bodies,
and, in certain rapture,
I touched the living hems
of their capacious robes, ore-twined.
As they went by, the coarse feathers
of their large wings touched my forehead.

When I plunged down, the walls
of the sky rumbling all around me,
I fell upon the nimble spokes
of the air cleaving apart,
I still saw their luminous corners
flaring up on the mountain ridge,
then, as the plunging slowed,
I circled round the lower waters.

The current carries my blackening
body like blind ash,
the oily mineral water
raises me in its thickly woven basket,
and while the measure of the barren

night sea blares its rhythm unceasingly,
in the heights, drifting away,
I still hear the rustle of their wings.

Translated by Ottilie Mulzet

FALLEN ANGEL

Down there, in the depths of the depths
there is built the only land
where the feet of the wicked
are washed by tears of mercy.

Poor things. Ravaged by crime
are their wonderful ancient faces.
Whosever is this compassion,
has walked into hell with them.

Translated by Ottilie Mulzet

COMPANION

Trailing my steps,
lurking nearby, is love,
lying low beside a wall,
in every street nook hiding.

Following me without a trace
as big as one shadow,
whoever saw me would think
I'm here all by myself.

No matter where I go,
stepping behind, stepping in front,
awaiting me on the other side,
following me with stealth.

Translated by Ottilie Mulzet

UNKNOWN

In the darkness the ocean rises,
with unknown torture arrives,
hardly any shore offers protection,
this far I have come. Odium, odium.

I, who sufficed for myself,
must I endure being seized,
onto the black waves thrown,
as looming above, they devour me?

I have no other love but the earth,
the sky—help me, struggle with me,
do not forsake me, o this one world,
for no other love have I. So it shall be.

Translated by Ottilie Mulzet

RESURRECTION

The raised arms, ready to strike
fall when I approach them,
on every face there is shock,
people avoid me, turn away.

For I lay there among the others,
under the quicklime, in fraying armies,
but then some kind of force came along,
pulled me away.

Now I walk again. I have no path,
but above me is the sweet clear sky,
beneath me unfolds the living earth,
I feel his hand upon my shoulder.

Translated by Ottilie Mulzet

HOME

The lands disappear forevermore,
forevermore the sea does vanish,
like ebbing water, they leave me to myself,
villages never seen floating away.

My shelter is built here, from this wood,
the corners and the walls about to be made.
Let not these columns collapse
but grow tall, become my safe abode.

Translated by Ottilie Mulzet

PUBLIC GARDEN

Ever since the mornings stopped,
twilight never arrives,
its gold ever more densely
weighs down upon the leaves.

From the picture swells out
inner and outer illumination
its spaces about to collapse
under the relentless sun's burden.

Suspended among my memories,
swaying like bulging sacks,
tightened until bursting
are those hours glowing brightly.

Beneath brimstone-yellow plane trees
upon foliage they lie,
never ascending from that place,
the two lovers never rise.

Translated by Ottilie Mulzet

RAIN

The rain was cascading down,
onto the roofs, the walls,
illuminated in eternal rain
the lovers' faces, uncovered.

From doorway to doorway,
from bench to bench, for weeks on end,
the skies grew heavy above,
the coat covering them, drenched.

Drenched was every street,
the empty forests, the bridges,
around them the buildings' storeys,
heated walls, dry inner rooms.

For them there were only termini,
only uninhabited gardens,
only plunging illumination,
only rain and cold.

The warmth will seep from the stove,
as well as from people's abodes,
but there will remain, like the moon,
the illumination of their uncovered faces.

Translated by Ottilie Mulzet

SEVEN FAIRY TALES

I

Above the clouds, arabesques, a ledge
where the autumn princess is looking out.
She waits for her bridegroom in vain,
the wooden chest has flown away.

II

Little Red Riding Hood skips through the woods,
unsuspecting, goes where she shouldn't,
poor thing walks right into the trap,
Little Red Riding Hood skips through the woods.

III

Snow White, you're the fairest of all!
If they find out, you will be killed.
But you're taken in by seven true dwarves
And your stepmother avoids the mirror.

IV

Little duck swims in a little lake,
from shore to shore quickly floating.
Above her are gigantic wings,
the centuries' swans ascend.

V

When I chop off one head,
three sprout in its place.
That too I will chop off:
My dragon, you won't escape.

VI

I carried him to the shore
and I never spoke a word,
I walked on the knife's blade for him,
yet he paid me no heed.

VII

Once upon a time a prince set off,
he went to seek the truth.
By the time the truth was found,
so many princes had walked that path.

Translated by Ottilie Mulzet

PELICAN

Like the pelican, I feed the young,
the disciples of my own happiness.
My days are ever more illuminated,
while I am ever more invisible.

Translated by Ottilie Mulzet

THIRTY

As you are now, so you will remain.
Your face, your eyes, will stay the same.
Low tide will come for flesh as for foam,
but these features will not change.

What exists now will still be seen,
surplus falling away without a trace,
the mountain-soil carried down by the days,
while the living are pervaded by the dead.

Translated by Ottilie Mulzet

MADONNA

Holder of light without light,
a hollow figure,
whose movements could not be
more still.

A sombre mother,
her son so bright,
euphoria
after depression.

Translated by Ottilie Mulzet

JANUARY

To breathe
as one can
breath moves
in the air

In itself, too,
should be enough
to survive
on one breath

Stopping above
a wintry face
steam unfurling
its white semicircle

Translated by Ottilie Mulzet

JULY

Because every movement above
the earth's surface
the long nights, white days
brings ever closer

Brings ever closer the long
white days
ever closer that which you are
that which I am

Translated by Ottilie Mulzet

AN EVENING

A city above the river
as the trees
as through ever more untraversable
terrain

The windows the roofs as
they grow ever heavier
in onslaughts darkening
with me with you

Translated by Ottilie Mulzet

THE PLACE

Instead of so many vanishing
possibilities
to reach that one time
that one place

To finally reach that place
where one is called
where—incomprehensibly
where—happily

Translated by Ottilie Mulzet

A DRAWING

Only a few
darkened lines:
hardly leaving behind
something of itself

Maybe a bridge:
a fragment
curving above
as if a tree branch

Only this tree branch
and half a bridge:
all around, surface, emancipated,
a testament

Translated by Ottilie Mulzet

GOING FARTHER

When the elements binding material
come undone
the resident within may no longer
be transformed

what has been reached lies in front
what was in vain drifts aside
life is forced to confront
its state of torso-being

The stumps of absence
yanked into empty convulsions
pulled back by the direction
of lost possibilities

But all that was realized
yearns to clutch at something else
always urging farther, farther
beyond, to a more complete self

Translated by Ottilie Mulzet

THE FOREST

The forest in spring is completely new,
its branches unencumbered by weight,
only feather-light floating green,
only tiny buds, only sprouting leaves.

The summer forest's foliage, colossal.
Hearken the whisper of deep green,
as below, half asleep, you lie
in the coolness of the clearing.

The autumn forest, most beautiful of all.
Yellow-red leafage turning,
its lantern light illuminates
until the fall of evening.

Silent is the winter forest.
Snow, snow, on the trees, the ground,
who falls into the snow's embrace,
shall ever see it falling from above.

Translated by Ottilie Mulzet

BREATH

Its faithfulness is now
the greatest
of warmth
while I still live

Although its sanctuary
lies ever more
distant, still
it reaches over here

so gently, as
if breath
might pervade
this brittle land

Translated by Ottilie Mulzet

CATARACT

Cleave from my eye, Lord,
a cataract, if it grew there
so I can see again who you once were
so I can see where the illumination, the altar

Translated by Ottilie Mulzet

SNOW

If it snows If the snow falls
onto the ground if the snow falls down
onto the wounded lowlands then
there shall arise a higher formation

Translated by Ottilie Mulzet

ZSUZSA TAKÁCS

(1938–)

ANIMA

Soul, don't peer into our human night!
Everywhere you'll hear the wailing of the creatures.
I know you are alone, exiled far from home,
forced to live in darkness.
Our darkness weeps out of the earth at you
like severed heads living still and crying.
And you try to recall the light
but your memory forsakes you.
You, free spirit, winged and chill,
you glance at us and turn away with a shudder.
We cover the mud with our kisses
and however miserable a spot on earth it is
we call it home.
And after this idiotic slobbering you're seized with anxiety;
your heaven doesn't exist, it's merely a product of your imagination,
you are forced, as everyone tells you, to live
your entire botched life here.
This overpopulated place is made for you to rot in—
where the most innocent blade of grass must also rot,
where the blade triumphant rises from corruption—
and murderous joys haunt you,
something is drawn from you,
you will grow dry, prickly, wounding.

. . .

What has happened to make this town,
the scene of my failure, so important to me.
I kneel at piles of rubbish people have thrown out
and make a new world from what I find there.
I envy the simple directness of the body,
I thirst for the touch of skin
as my soul once thirsted for a sight of God.
I tread the dim paths of a woman about her business
who earns her crust by the sweat of her brow,
who goes to have her hair done and looks
with fear at her reflection in the mirror,
who writes letters and believes it's her poems
addressing the world.
I am with her on her walks through the poisoned air,
lost in her yearnings and desires
as she watches a man's mouth,
I, immortal soul, am forced to share
a body with her.
But at night, when it's time
for moonlit contemplation,
I yank the loose stake from the ground,
attach it to my chain and drag it round
the infinite yard, and let those upstairs
hear that terrible clatter, breaking down the gate,
running through bog and brake, bloody voiced,
as if it had sliced my back open,
as if the iron had punctured my intestines,
rushing till I gasp for breath, pausing
only till I can start again, cursing
the verdict, which isn't my verdict,
the destiny, which isn't my destiny,
but some alien's desire.

While it dreams I take revenge on the body
I mock its hasty incomplete encounters,
I plant skeletal deathcamp trees in its forest places,
I disguise its loves with a wolfish mask,
and roll up its heaven
like a withered scroll.

. . .

If you have time to spare, if you have a word for me,
if you raise your eyes to your imagined God,
if you can close your imagined eyes,
to such a blaze of light,
if you're blinded by that which I cannot see,
intercede for me!
At the bottom of the jasper stairs, before
the carpet with its golden weave I stand
dumb among the hallelujah choir,
THE SOUL'S FANTASY, THE BODY.
My movement has fractured the air,
my heels have crushed the secret signs,
in sickness, at vigil, at fast,
in disgrace, as cheat,
as stranger and deathdesirer
as one beaten but not destroyed, I beg.

. . .

I gladly surrender my bloody roses
I happily extinguish the bright torch of my eyes,
my laughter full of brilliant teeth dies away,
I do not tremble before my chosen one,
when he takes the flower from my hand,
when he wipes the hours from my face,

I reserve only that hour of terminal pallor
when my lovestruck child hides it from my eyes,
drawing the final jubilant pictures of the Place
into a vibrating membrane, so she should give birth
once more in disgrace and delight.
When the body clads itself in incorruptibility,
the temporal in the eternal,
when Earth grows bleak and desolate again.

Translated by George Szirtes

THE LOVELIEST MOVEMENT

Whatever is forced to join together
is sure to fall apart. No need to fight
it anymore, things come to pieces just

as I intended, link and chain divide.
(I failed to adjust, I must confess
although, God knows, how hard I tried.)

Leaf, how tenderly you dropped onto
the surface of the water. More tenderly
than any lover on the sex of the beloved.

Leaf, thank you, of all-movements it was the loveliest,
neither a mingling nor a tremor of the breast.
It was of all movements the loveliest.

Translated by George Szirtes

TO LEAVE

the crowded hall as the applause reaches
its climax, just as the world-weary clowns
are performing their brief routines,

not to sit up for their endless tricks,
to break the enthusiastic ranks,
to reclaim your coat, your hat, your umbrella

from the ecstatic attendant for a dime,
then set out across town, just as they
are shifting scenes but the set isn't yet ready

and the hours too stand still, and your only
companion is the smell of disinfectant
which floats down each street of the plague-stricken town.

Translated by George Szirtes

CONTINUATION

not to ring anyone (in any case the plants
will outgrow their pots and push
windows open leaning out-over the street),

not to take revenge, but not to take it
lying down either, not to cure your toothache
nor your inflamed retina, your leukaemia,

not to open the doors to the fire brigade though the house is burning,
not to snatch at straws when you are drowning,
to turn back from the detested door

at the moment of arrival. Not to look ahead
while walking, but backwards only. To bear the lash.
Then a leaf may fall onto the surface of the lake.

Translated by George Szirtes

REFURBISHMENT

Some slips and vests, the sticky blouses, jumpers
shrunk or stretched, that prickly woollen
waistcoat, a lot of unwanted stuff
picked up at sales, that skirt too easily creased,
soaked walking boots in which
my cracked heel used regularly to bleed,
paper tissues in a chequered pocket,
the blown pages of an Updike dropped in a bath,
ink-stain, grease-stain, heart-stains
on discarded rags. 'A prosodic approach to the translation
of Lorca', offprint in eighty-seven copies.
A white tie mourning with a dirty edge.
Second rate authors, duplicate copies, prescriptions
not collected, an empty notebook with the word DIARY
silver-embossed on the cover, children's bathing towels.
a one-week luncheon voucher dated seventy-three
(each day I dined with someone else)
a dried ink cartridge, in which
is written the terrible truth:
farewell my youth.

I sit before the open doors
of the wardrobe, while workmen rip
the house apart, and twenty years spin by.
The inflatable paddling pool, stuck together now,
the Italian gymslip which fitted years ago,

and a hospital report (ab. incompl.) slips
from the silk pocket of a sun bleached denim handbag,
my brows could be thinking of that May morning.
            Clods of earth are falling
like plaster in the renovated flat.
I sit entombed within myself, picking at
the musty grapes of autumns past.
And I can hear the neighbours arriving, but no one
crosses the mountain of rubble. Dust flies, creeps
under doors. I might once have feared cockroaches
but their thousand feet are not so fearsome now.
I manage among the sounds of demolition.
Clothes unmade and yet already ruined
flap on the clothesline of the future.
I writhe in sweaty man-made fibres and sandals.
Undeveloped rolls of film make me laugh
with ever greater abandon.
Hoarded addresses, unrecognized telephone numbers
bulge in tomorrow's diary which slips behind
a drawer and I cannot find it again,
only paper bubbling from jammed drawers
I've tried to force open.
To have been dwarfs in Lilliput,
what is that to the millennia?
—Our lives, that's all.
                              Our one hand gropes about
our sentimental heart. Our laced-up feet, like Magritte shoes,
wait for permission to enter the secret gate.
Our eyes, cracked with use, drop the odd stone
or tear on stitched-up uncomplaining lips.
Wrinkled necks of silk hiss in the resurrected wind.
A sagging lacy breast light like a butterfly
on an ancient bony shoulder. Their blood

was fire in a bottle of scent.
I can still start over again, wrote the
hand, slowly drowning, on the sun-worn horizon
of the fading shore.
                                        The day was long ago.
                                        If non-existence proves possible
under such fertile soil, I may forgive you.

Translated by George Szirtes

A HAT

How perfect it is, this hat,
hung on the copper hook next to my own.
It's green but of a rather subtle shade,
the ribbon black, threaded through with gold.
How many terrible thoughts have brewed beneath it,
what thoughts have dashed themselves to death within it.
Surely it has passed from father to son.
It disturbs me like some kind of family heirloom.
It's rather tight but has been brushed to a shine.
Just looking at it the blood drains from my face.
Its owner is a swollen-faced fat man
who will eventually come to claim it,
and when he does I won't look, let him not see me.
I'd like him to put it on as he was leaving,
but I'm sure he'll stand there and take a look around,
and no one will fail to rise in honour of him.
I wish I could forget that I have met him
or that I might have to meet him again.
If possible let him have no family,
nor dog that he could put in a sack and beat.
If he's a judge, let me not come before him.
If he gets violent, let his first blow be fatal.

Translated by George Szirtes

THE ADORATION OF THE BODY

When they were making love for the last time
and, wide-eyed, she watched herself doing it,
squirming with lust, her whole face
twisted, practically screaming with
excitement, with the ecstasy
of annihilation, of being annihilated,
of destruction, of the burning of bridges,
the putting of a spoke in the wheel of time,
of bending time's own spokes, the dance
of metallic slivers piercing their skin, the thousand
cuts in what tied them together, the final
slicing apart, the recognition of the familiar strangeness
of the body falling on her body, of movements
that radiated such utter resolution, she cried for the joy
of the sigh-like departure of love from their flesh,
she cried because she felt it was appropriate for
what they were punishing, that months-long sense,
the insidious pain spreading through everything, the soul.

Translated by George Szirtes

OUR MASTER'S ABSENCE

The Master was away and it was pointless waiting
to be let in. One of us eventually
plucked up courage to enter the open house
but as the dogs drew closer, howling, a hand gripped
and captured him. Fear unhinged him,
and he lost control, breaking and wrecking things,
until he escaped through a smashed picture window
and joined us. The Master called us to account.
We trembled before him and lied our heads off,
but never revealed the rebel's name to him.
We are, after all, servants, and easily offended.
Our self-regard is ridiculous in his presence.

Translated by George Szirtes

FROM GRAMMAR FOR ADVANCED STUDENTS

DEDICATION

To all those who cannot sleep for pain and at night circle aimlessly in their rooms, sit in the same place or, if unable to, lie on the crumpled sheets with eyes closed or wide open and try to trick the blurry mix of sensations and, appealing to time's helping hand, wait for the salvation of the morning. To all those who place poultices or plasters on their sore body, take some Contramal or refuse to take it, trying to go off it rather, so they may keep their consciousness clear the longest possible. To those who give in to, or rebel against suffering and so become drug dependent. To all who are wept for or not wept for, with whom the others are patient or impatient, who cling to a doorsill, a car door-handle, the staircase railings, to strange or familiar arms and who, although at an immeasurable distance from the healthy, turn to them with forgiving mercy and worried love.

TWELVE EXPERIMENTS

(1) *Travellers' supper*
Last supper offered by
travellers on the downtown roof
terrace beneath green sun blinds
in stifling heat. Far beyond your
reach and mine, my darlings,
my sweaty palm bears aloft
the cut crystal wineglass of farewell.

(2) *Please,*
may the threatening movement be
suspended. Not that it's been much good
so far. May the throat rest uncut! This way
I'll be able to learn this and that. Please, may
the punctual terror of lightbulbs burning at night
be delayed yet.

(3) *I have considered*
Tossed among the gnashing teeth
of air I have considered what I did
wrong. I do not hold myself
guilty. Still, I wholeheartedly regret
if I have ever offended you,
and readily take my place
among the waiting.

(4) *We who have slept*

We who have slept in self-forgetfulness,
loose lids over the Watchful Eye,
are now startled as if by a scream
at the first bird call at dawn
and rinse ourselves. Then, returning into our
bodies, we descend into reality's fearful
circles by the ramshackle elevator.

(5) *Padlock*

Adieu, my lost world!
I remain to the very end, but they have drugged me.
The lock springs open, riddle and solution
click into one another. I keep spinning
the crushing padlock: I feel a feather's
weight only. Stretching my wings, I flap
around my belongings.

(6) *The surgeon*

After the impeccable opening,
accompanied by the birds' jubilee,
the clean-shaven man appears.
His blue eyes rise slowly in their
sockets: sun in the sky. He cannot fail
to see the root of woes. He descends
from a tower, lightning bolts in his hand.

(7) *Defeating the Monster*

To call the Monster by its name,
however tedious, to utter
its cawing syllables: Cancer.
May it end up in the litterbin

under the circumstances it deserves
while we rest amid the pillows
of Your palm full of nooks and crannies.

(8) *I tried to resist*
I tried to resist, in vain.
Finally the extra painkiller
starts working, but the switched-off
fluorescent light continues burning under
my eyelids. The contours
of operating tables quiver and dissolve
before tranquillity takes hold of me.

(9) *Time*
During the five-and-a-half days that last for weeks
until the poison in the infusion starts
working on me, the eye inside my brain
observes how the mountain built
of debris crumbles slowly.
I should perhaps put on a mask,
so that you won't be frightened by me.

(10) *Imaginings*
As on a chess board, the poison moves
on my scalp among the light and dark thoughts,
removing my hair. I go to swim once more
before my death. May my limbs smelling
of water bless you, Lord! *May you be blessed by our*
pure and humble sister, water. That I need not
stand soiled before Your eyes.

(11) *Anyone can practice*
Anyone can practise on me
the corporal acts of mercy.
They can touch my shoulder. Or, drowning
their tears in coughs, can knock over
a glass as they rush out footless
the moment they glimpse
the bleeding crescents of my nails.

(12) *So many attempts*
Post-mortem lights of the shortening
afternoon. From a pulled-down car
window splinters of disco music
crash into the traffic. The one climbing
back from the pit stands up
after so many diligent
attempts. Summer is over. She is cold.

GOING ON

(13) *On a revolving stage*
I have to stand on a revolving stage
motionless, you thought. If I can stand it,
I can surrender to weakness.
I can weep on all kinds of shoulders
and relate what protective headgear
we had to wear during treatment, so that
our faces would not be scorched at least.

(14) *Comparison*
'Don't compare my suffering to another's!'
I requested. I'll compare it myself if I will
to Christ's five wounds, or to the journey through hell
of the caretaker's wife, who was cured in the end.
Do not enlist names for whose sake
I should submissively endure the torments
of those poisoned by radiation.

(15) *Convalescence*
Did the summer of my homelessness
leave its marks on my face, I asked.
My glass is dark, I cannot tell.
My thankfulness sweeps over the broken
leaves piled up, left from last year,
in front of porches. Where shall I stand,
so that I won't scare you away?

(16) *Embrace*

Shall the dry complaint engraved
in my skin touch your skin? I fear
my sweat-drops give me away.
Weigh the consequences carefully.
Whatever you decide, you are right.
Farther from you, or nearer:
I'll stand where you want me to stand.

ABYSS AND HOPE

(17) *The pitch-black point*
Hissing into the abyss, condensing
into a sole pitch-black point, the leftover
world falls, they say, as the body's
excretions fall into the common
pit. But You have seen that man
is poorly when alone.
So, my Lord, they're all wrong.

(18) *My home*
Then no sound came from my throat.
A street vendor kept following me, I wanted
to say no, I wasn't buying any towels
for my bathroom, tablecloths for the kitchen,
but my throat emitted only a pathetic
screech. What could I have told her
that has not been heard yet?

(19) *Every place*
Isn't every place my home? The strange
pillow under my sticky hair? Isn't
the 1.90 by 0.80 metre bed
my own? Does the window of the ward not
look on the windows of neighbouring houses
or on an empty plot, deeply moved, as we two
look now into one another's eyes?

(20) *All His angels*

Her long deceased parents stood by the table,
wiping off her forehead or holding
the surgeon's elbow when he cut and
sutured, for five hours while the family
were arguing or comforting each other
in front of the operating theatre. They listened to
the earthly reasoning and smiled indulgently.

Translated by Erika Mihálycsa

DEDICATION: IN MEMORY OF MY PARENTS

If my father, as mayor of the town, didn't stand in front of the Arrow Cross men who were about to loot a fabric shop, to tell them, with his service revolver in his right hand and his wallet in his left, to take the wallet but better not break into the store or else he'll shoot, because it was his duty to protect the property of citizens of the town who were called up for labour service—if father didn't do that, I would have fled the family home, to remind myself of the stories I had heard about better times, when Roman law still commanded respect in the legal profession and among the people. If my mother didn't bend over her children so as to absorb with her body pieces of the window that was shattered by a bullet, I would have said: *How dark it is here!* as I stepped up to her sickbed in her room with its swing-out window, in the projects. If my father, pale with anger, didn't go after the looting soldier, telling him to take everything but give back my doll, then, twenty years later, while running down the stairs like crazy, I would have almost knocked over the cleaning woman who with pail and mop would have been in a hurry to get to our place. If mother didn't give blood so she could use the money to buy a pair of shoes for my kid brother, I would have asked: *Did you close the window too?* while standing in that stuffy room which would have been locked in, put in the stocks, as it were, by a brick wall looming in the neighbouring yard. If during father's detention she didn't provide for us by stitching shoulder pads; if in March of '57 she took the outstretched hand of a member of the security police and hearing him complimenting her on her good looks, even smiled involuntarily, just before father was herded into their heavily curtained Pobeda car, then, like a starveling grabbing the last bite, I would have grabbed the railing that separated our street from the river, and leaped over it. But like this, under the weight of the love and gratitude I felt for them, I sat in the world's big top, all the way up, my face red and white, my eyes fixed on the skinny equestrienne who was goaded on by the ruthless circus director's cracking whip, amid the unceasing blare of the band, the whirr of fans and the spectators' thunderous applause. It could well have been drops of my own sweat and blood that were soaked up by the insatiable sand in that ring, but I applauded the child-bodied lady's act just the same, so as not to take the fun out of our entertainment. *Seek the one and only Moon and Sun that will light up infinity just for you*, the circus fanfares blasted in my ear; and if in my loneliness I found my relatives among the clowns, the trapeze artists, the lion tamers and the caged lions, and cried in tight, tiled corners, I had to concede that if there's one, there can be two or three, and if two, then six or six hundred billion Moons and Suns in the sky, while behind the swing-out window of our death chamber, glistening with the waxy coat of birth, a single one rises from the ocean. Between the source of light and the place where we stand we cannot see everything at once, in our eyes the nearest star is the same as it was years ago. And if all of a sudden every light source was extinguished, we would keep staring for centuries at something that ceased to exist ages ago. The young child, whose hand the two of you held, sniffed around like a dog in a familiar doorway, and holding her head heavy with wise mysteries on her thin neck, sucked into her wide eyes a world rich and frightful.

Translated by Ivan Sanders

PREMONITIONS OF MOURNING (SELECTIONS)

I STARTED AWAKE

I started awake when a door slammed,
seized by terror that you died that instant
and the gust of wind banged the door left
open. Was it you who left it deliberately
open, to let me know the time of your departure?
It was three in the morning. The wings
of two black moths brushed across my face
as I walked around the apartment: two
noxious heralds. One I killed,
it crumbled in my handkerchief
and stained the death-white wall.
The other made its nest in my
heart, lays eggs from which the days
ahead are slowly hatching.

MACHINES DO

Machines do your breathing, your
sleeping. You lie with eyes closed,
clean shaven under the gaze of your wretched
visitors. In the whole ward you are
the most beautiful. Your sinewy arm,
well-proportioned chest are revealed to us.
Though I dressed in white, against my
will my tears well up.

FOR SEVENTEEN DAYS

For seventeen days you've been sleeping. While I was
by your bedside a gust of wind reached in
the window left open at home and knocked
over the floor lamp I received from
you. Let everything perish, that is its will.

TWENTY-THREE DAYS

For twenty-three days
you've been laid out for us in the snow-white ward
freezing and sweating,
so we may go on our pointless
errands. You lie,
your dark eyelashes flutter yet

unable to lift your heavy
eyelid, your gaze the green
bird will not settle
on us.

FROM NOW ON

From now on dark falls earlier.
At six in the morning the streets are dark.
Night glows with cold light.
Shades drift, the blind
walk side by side.

IF ANYBODY TOUCHED ME

If anybody touched me now, their freezing
hands would pull away at once.
I stand, moonlit shade on the lamp-
lit street, waiting to be let in.
Black geraniums the size of a child's
head beckon in a window. The tears of
a sprinkling can trickle down on them.

THE TIME COMES

The time comes when you've had enough.
There will be tears I dreaded long
in advance, when the Lord of Heaven
places you in His hall of statues—
so there were. Outside, the sun is shining.

POSTSCRIPT

Like one deranged, the tram clangs
up and down the streets, looking
for someone lost in the night.
It picks up some discarded rags
and drops them again. A clatter.
Snow frozen to splinters.

Translated by Erika Mihálycsa

IF WE INDEED HAVE SOULS

to András Visky

It has no single form. And that's the point!
Can we trust in that which constantly changes
its appearance? In Blind Hope? It could be
a beggar on the street corner, or a young woman,
servant to a house, marched off to Auschwitz
together with her masters, to the Danube Delta
or Vorkuta where she remains in service to them,
digging out roots from under the snow or going through
the rubbish. Ancients are there to tell us stories
to protect the soul in us, if we indeed have souls
and are not merely creatures perpetuating our species.

Should night last not the usual eight hours, but
continue for weeks or years or even whole decades,
so that when the sun appears it's only by mistake,
would we still trust it? Pretty soon
disaster tourists
arrive in air-conditioned buses to visit our
disaster-stricken city,
and our tyrant's pet gelding
conducts them round the luxury hotel and turns on
taps of gold,—though that's not what they paid for,
they say, as they beat the table demanding whisky
in our Potemkin village—no, they want to meet us.

Do we have rights, and soap, do we have books,
hospitals, schools, and paid overtime? they ask.
They're particularly keen to know about our
orphanages because they have seen others elsewhere
and those remain their fondest memory.
And would we like to travel the way they do?
They mention a tsunami in Asia and show us photos
of themselves in such places, as they explain,
with Sony camcorders round their necks among
bodies buried in mud. They offer us chairs
and want to share their salmon with us, while we
stand gawping in the restaurant, caught on CCTV,

eyes popping out, not touching the food. If their looking
disturbs us, they say, they can turn away but we are
constantly being looked at, we answer, and gaze at them,
admiring their beauty.
Do you still have hope,
they ask us,
and we recall the beggar on Petőfi corner
and the young woman who accompanied us to Auschwitz,
the Danube Delta, and Vorkuta, and their cameras click and flash
and then to make sure they won't confuse us with others,
they carefully note the time and place of their visit.

Translated by George Szirtes

ACCEPT!

You'd interfere in everything!—my companion
Blind Hope snapped. His harsh tone took me aback.
Only in life and death, I answered, overcome
by a spirit of rebellious defiance.
No giving up, I kept repeating to myself. We had been
waiting since eight in front of the paediatric
oncology's operating theatre. At long last a surgeon
came out and turned to a man chosen at random.

I was glad he didn't pick me, for he no longer
wore his mask: his face was naked
and ominous. He passed on the dismal news, bowed
slightly, waited, then turned and left the man alone.
God damn!—the Sacrificial Lamb, the (dead) child's
father wailed all of a sudden, but his voice broke,
his tears were thickly streaming, he slid down
on the empty bench. My companion stepped over to him.

Who does he think he is, to address him like that?!
He reached out to the man's shoulder, but with one
yank, he tore off and threw this touch
from him. Accept it! Accept it!—my companion
said, standing so close, as if he were

by my side. But I am
no saint!—the man screamed. You are,
all of you—Blind Hope replied.

Translated by Erika Mihálycsa

WITH BLIND HOPE IN A CAFÉ

I was sitting on the avenue
at the tilting table of a recently opened
café, conversing with Blind Hope.
He asked: what are the streets like in the early spring?—he asked.
I answered: dirty, last year's fallen leaves
are still rotting away beneath the walls.
And the people's faces?
Better not to know—I said. They eye
each another wickedly, and you can hear for yourself,
for you are blind not deaf, what filthy language they use.
And what kind of clothes do they wear?—he pressed on.

I listened to him, it began to rain, rattling
down on the awning above our heads.
It rained, but the sun was relentlessly shining.
Shall I talk to him about the torn jeans?
doesn't he have enough on his hands already? about
the shapeless, soiled plastic sneakers? The cars
splashed the pavement with mud. I wanted to pay.
He asked me to stay. He hears angels
treading, he said, hears their bare soles flitting
as they walk above the water in shining clothes.
He said he could feel the sea drops on his face.

Translated by Erika Mihálycsa

BLIND HOPE WEAKENING

I wanted to meet Blind Hope,
asked him to choose a suitable place,
Last Judgement Square in Budapest for instance,
or some sinking island from where no passage
leads back. The inside of a crystal globe. A night
shelter where somebody is clubbed to death.
He should admit that his hopefulness was silly.
False and stomach-turningly pink like himself.
I wanted to hurl some deadly insult at him
for having duped me for so many decades.

That while the others fell, I was left standing,
for there is something loathsome in survival.
My cell phone trembled and turned pale in my hand
at the rudeness with which I spoke to him.
You rotten beast!—my voice shrieked, while my eyes
dropped quick tears of self-pity. He apologized
for not having the time.
He receives hundreds of emergency
calls like mine every day, he said. And that he
himself is on the verge of collapse.

Translated by Erika Mihálycsa

IN SEPTEMBER '43

The man deported from Maramaros saw
Kafka. As if windblown, he swung
here and there, while we were standing on the
Appelplatz, he swore, and that he was
ghostly, like one drawn with chalk
into the dark. I have survived more adverse
times already, Kafka told him—so he said—

and that in his dream he was with Milena
in Kaffee Union, and at their table, beneath
the leaf-framed mirror, sat a man looking like
Dostoevsky with a girl looking like
Milena, correcting a manuscript. And that
he'd never believed in himself so much
as in that September nineteen

forty-three. The man from Maramaros
added that, because his loose teeth
were shifting, Kafka had learnt
to speak with his bleeding lips closed,
'as if his thoughts were voicing'.
He was none other than Blind
Hope, made flesh.

Translated by Erika Mihálycsa

ZSÓFIA BALLA

(1949–)

FLOWERS

They rang the bell, just stepped into the house,
the flowers did, and into the vase.

They looked around, liked the flat,
it kept them busy,
and nothing else mattered.

But they were used to
flowering as they
wanted
and here, lo,
their stalks are cut daily.
Their dreams are clipped.
Put in cold water every morning,
they are forced to flower anew
and do it eagerly.

They got tired of it.
Didn't need wonders.
Grew to hate
the bright rooms.
From spite, they gave no scent.
Conspiring to wither, they went.

Translated by Anna Bentley

IN THE OTHER WING OF THE PALACE

I write on gilt paper,
while the chorus cowers below,
young women preening
in fire-warmth.
When the thick lump of time
masses in the throat,
and silence circles in space,
troubled, falling to the wall.

Mingling among the props
fishes howling, pulling,
and I stand stubbornly,
weeping and silent.
If we were to speak, the mother-of-pearl-
light-words would float
up above each other. Comprehending
nothing from the past.

Translated by Ottilie Mulzet

MORNING PRAYER

Winter sunlight sits hesitantly on the window's surface,
behind the marble dusk-clouded fog;
on the windowsill, frost's iron teeth bite
into half a squash, coffee's pungent fragrance bubbles.
Ha! Once again the turning of time,
this is Winter's scent,
just like the old days!—
The kitchen floor is excited as it dries:
May all your wishes come to be.

Translated by Ottilie Mulzet

ON THE EDGES

I stand on the edge of a rug: before me tall, slender
kings proceed, embracing me around my waist,
amorous dead fathers. Music blossoms,
behind me lightning flashes, softly,
a slender bolt—I stand, resigned,
within slow hissing sounds. To lose forever
who has not come with me this far; this is the Island's end,
from here on in, there is only freezing cement.
The soles of my feet are bare.

Translated by Ottilie Mulzet

DESCENT TO HELL

How many times will you die, Father, after this
how shall I carry you?
When you died for the first time, I laughed
in play—a foolish child;

no premonition ever reached me.
Now every silence—enclosed
with this laughter, with
my age of unknowing—is too small.

Each one of my memories buries you anew,
finally pushing you onto the ark of souls;
Charon jumped out and he's laughing!
Eternally rowing between two shores.

I grew up without you; like that tree
the grows tall even bearing the trace of the axe.
In my childishness I ask: tell me, Father,
within me, do you remember yourself?

Translated by Ottilie Mulzet

THE ROSE

for Csaba Báthori

I

Still a few days for us to look at each other.
A momentary pause in our mutual falling.
The other's path will be grasped only by the one who falls.

Like a shell, the petals slowly come to pieces—
the taut stem whispers only of itself:
smoky triangles one after the other
gathering in ever more narrow circles—
or is it the peacock's eye coiling from within?
The eddying forms of petals,
murmuring, enclose what
the ripening rose conceals: the full,
tight middle.

Because that is what never opens.
Retreating before armies
wrapped in its secret.
                    We will never know
what it might show deeper inside,
in the darkness of that vaulted space:
petals protecting, protecting and besieging.

Within the depths of the rose, another rose.

II

Only he that falls will know his place.

The rose is cooling here on the table—
but I'm afraid that soon it shall bow down, and fall,
tomorrow or today it will give up, for
it has opened until spinning, sprawling
like an upturned eye.
                                                            It stands,
splaying apart its petals, stems, leaves,
and now that it has opened and the end is near,
my gaze sweeps across it, imbibing greedily,
so that I can see it too, since it is already dying.
My gaze browses through its slippery gradients,
tasting them, taking measure—
groping, between what is closed: the voided cilium,
the petals' substance, silent cavity
of butterfly-powdered surface, its heat,
the rose's head held high.
                                                But for how long?

In vain do I warm my face with the rose's warmth—
Its fire wanes, flickers! Because only it,
only it fills me with joy! Neither its image, its likeness
nor its tidings, no! In vain do I bade it tarry,
the honey-coloured rose, as it sheds its light within
like a lamp, rustling like a dense,
vanilla-tinged wind—
While it is here—now!—drink the sight of it to its root.

What's the point in being eternal, if it no longer lives?

Translated by Ottilie Mulzet

SKY AND EARTH

Still visible, how the copper sky
is overgrown by rough clouds, graphite-grey,
like the flesh of wild game; above, a shaft of light
at times peeks out, then slackens, breaks.

The landscape turns around. A screaming train
on the horizon, the sky's burning does not cease—
fired enamel plating on its luminous planes,
halo refracted through beams of light.

We burrowed through the sanguineous century like worms:
the past collapses above a solitary tunnel.
History is camouflaged with rubble.
The lawn is heated by the underworld's logwood-dead.
As, from the depths, I reach the sky's lower edge
pitilessly rumbling away from my own life,
pain, words, landscapes—everything so cold:
before my face the grey cloud-blade falls.

Translated by Ottilie Mulzet

THE THIRD TALE

All afterlives are suspect. Silence is just
A dubious side street: denial comes of it.
The rubble and smoke of what combusts
Turns Legend and Bible into holy writ.

What happened? Two millennia are too short
To know. Job carved it on the bone. The dead inherit.
Fatal stray bullets orbit the ether. God holds court.
Only the wicked discourse upon merit.

They weigh you up, the legions of the dead.

Your love is a bitter salt. There is no freedom
in the other's body—anxiety will not refine
A passion: you must keep vigil, watch
Like a naked mirror. Do not mistake their sign
Or confuse them with dreams. Do not lose track of them.

You yourself cannot escape, though you come after.
If guiltless you know it's by merest chance alone.
Scandal is a greased slope that floods and smears.
It is only of them God speaks with me and of their ills.
He'd give his life to have their death undone.

Translated by George Szirtes

THE SIGN OF THE GOAT

Mummy dear,
look, here I sit
bound to earth, under the sign of the Goat
in damp and bitter cold,
inhaling the sunlight
so that I may row across
to you, where you live in the Fish.
The two signs are closer
then we are, we who the will
of the stars has shoved apart.

Even now you draw me to you
and far away I'm waiting
for the meeting of our houses
so we might find new strength.
Stand in the sweep of our orbits
and call me by my old name,
in words that no one but I
can understand. That's why I'm waiting.
No one but you can locate me
I alone am the one seeking you.

Only you can decipher my verse,
the open cage of my bird-tongue,
this plashy swallow-twitter.
Tell me, should I drop the half of it?

Dammit.
No, look at how neatly
We cling to each other
With conspiratorial giggles.

You come to me with rumours.
I've waited, how long have I waited:
lay your blotched hand
half poplar, half glass, on my head
my crown of five branches.

Translated by George Szirtes

AFTERWARDS

It would be good, after my death,
to get up, like after a boxing match.
From another existence, from the outside, to awkwardly
keep looking, see what's coming next:
how long will it last? diminution? illumination?
for who you are, what I am—
when does it flicker out, and is the *border*
a tumbling stone wall, or a string of membrane?
where does the *tunnel* come to an end?
was the picture in my mind's eye? and if I saw it,
when did it disappear, into what did it fade?

I don't know which was dream:
the fullness of my being, my destruction
now sparked, now extinguished.

I can still write, as I am alive.
It would be good not to fear—but I'm afraid,
because all is a lie in this constricted passage.
And fear cannot be pardoned.

I wish I could know what I only suspect,
the certainty of what is to come:
all that is concealed will open.

All that was connected is now a diluted pile.
What was revolving is now sluggish grain.
The shade is nimbler on the wall.
Do I hear the body of crackling
silence, the gnarled mass?
Because nothing holds together,
nothing by nothing led:
the cells, as if by magic,
let go of each other's hands.

The living body is the substance
of turning time—but now only its sheer
presence. Its transfiguration
is not magic or occult:

within the earthly points of two cast anchors
the beginning and the end glow, incandescent.
Although I crawled as far as the stars,
I am scorched to the bone by nothingness.

The beginning
                                is a river, from a drop of water.
Life only from life conceived.
Which blazing, flits across
thousands of years, a sustained
voice, an undying torch's likeness.
Like nightmares' liquid ghost-lights.

The end
                                also breaks into nothingness.
Death washes away the shore:
not a voice, but a lack: a plain
of silence, shrieking of intervals.
In the hospital corridor, a worn,

bespattered iron bucket—and
regression, a wistful sinking down.
The stars are losing their accustomed order.

What kind of strength broke out of me
so that from nonexistence, I shone?
From dark and empty space, finitude
receives me like a homeland.
Hissing, falling into iron dust,
marching across my entire life,
it pushes me, shoves me, tosses me again
into empty space, where I am received

by the bloody kerchief of threadbare dreams.
Another existence glimmers through the mottled flame.
From fulfilment, my melting decay.

The living to the living, the dead to the dead—
as they say. Who transgresses this will grow dizzy and fall.
Will be woven, by radiant darkness, into shadow.

And yet still, yet still
                                        the pine cone
which is myself, which I would only like to see,
afterwards; once it has died,
how its scales will open.

Translated by Ottilie Mulzet

IN CREATION

All was decided in my absence,
Yet nothing has been decided here below.
I draw the image of God for myself
I decide what must be absolutely so.

I no more miss his presence when exploring
the ancient cosmic order of twisted fate.
And yet he insists on punishing me so that I
May not redress what Gods themselves create.

Translated by George Szirtes

THE OBJECT

We take the object, our favourite objects, in our hands, feel our way round them, use them. But it isn't this that lends them significance. This only wastes them, thins them out.

The object multiplies under my gaze. My eyes complete it. Awareness, special attention. Relationship. The fact that it reminds me of something of vital importance. That because of this—while I feel my way around it, give it a name—I must write it down. So I may display it.

The poem leans for shelter in the object, lies down in its shadow, hides itself behind it. The poem is the gaze that takes in every tiny detail of the object, makes us know it without mentioning every one of its characteristics, only those that the intention behind comprehension and creation may bend to itself: the fountain's concept of rising and falling, the lingering at its apex, the idea of returning into itself. The poem establishes the transfiguration of fine spray in the silence of noise.

My object is the one my eyes pick out. The one from which I cannot free myself. They'll do with it what they used to do with horses, goblets, the contingent: they will bury what I have seen along with me.

Translated by George Szirtes

BARE TREES

How beautiful they are when bare, the trees,
when their foliage is all shot away.
Sketched to their minutest joints.
Their wing-drawings display a coal-smudged map.

My eye surveys them like my lover's
body, pausing to rummage by a nest . . .
Ancient beauty, expiring nakedness
opening a well between iron-forged sinews.

The tree stands tall to the sky, the barrel of a gun.
Blossoms vomiting, into spring, a fusillade.
The arrow of a bare branch rushes up to heaven,
aiming at the target of blind fate above.

Translated by Ottilie Mulzet

A HUNDRED YEARS AGO TOMORROW

A hundred years ago tomorrow, in Alsóróna
a peasant woman gave birth
to you, black-haired girl,
who later laboured with me.
They murdered that woman, family and all.
You returned. And every day you cry.

Many have nibbled at my numbered days,
whittling you all from me. Today too
I thought of you: of how you forgave
Dad. And others. Me in the end.

Nothing in a camp is forgivable.
Neither can I suffer for my own omissions—
what's fraying, there's no point in me poking
back: what's good is dead. Many sins still live.

You are beautiful, Mama, watchful, you smell good.
You are beautiful and far away.
As dust, as twigs, and on a road of tiny bone fragments
you spread under me the parts of your mother.

Translated by Anna Bentley

MY GRANDMOTHER IN AN OVAL FRAME

For as long as I live, your gaze is in my spine.
For as long as I live, you will always hurt.
You sit on a full bundle. Naked, you move
forward. The tautening light suffocates
the block of wax, serpentine electrical currents.
Your death slips away among many other shades of crushing weight.

The past curls like a scab. It holds no memory of harm.
You are not autumn foliage and it is not the star's revolution
that pulverizes you.
No sowing or reaping bursts forth, glad
for you, peasant woman with your canister of milk.
My fate never stops slapping me.
Your life is a bat's wing, it trembles above.

Winged smoke is cast, ashes of time-smudge fall.
I see your hand as it rests
on your knee, your wedding band cuts into your finger.
Can I feel the ache of what I do not know?
A face whose story presses close to mine.

Drawn-out howling obscures
your grandchildren from you. The future,
if you can't touch it, disintegrates upon the living,
rending itself in rage. Your nonexistence points at me,
sniper floating on a ray, you.

What kind of family took you in?
I cannot bear to release that which has fallen.
Perhaps cessation is appropriate
to the order of life. But what kind of death
to add to it? In the dark wicker of my time
light and shadows are kicking about.

Translated by Ottilie Mulzet

OLD CHORALE

Forgive me, for I was born.
But why, my God, do you not reign within?

The padded cell in which I'm flailing,
is my body. How can I be free in flesh?

I'm writhing, all I am is being torn:
I grab your scent, my nails clatter on tin.

I am your ripened distance, singed stone:
I follow your trace like an extinct star.

Eternity's not long enough to reach you,
while honeyed anguish is your spittle.

I stretched out to you my hand, with song—yet
was it not inscrutable, your plan?

The entreating eulogy you hear with joy
—while letting every planet, every singer fall.

Translated by Ottilie Mulzet

THE TWO HALVES OF LIFE (FRAGMENTS FOR MIKLÓS GÁSPÁR TAMÁS) (SELECTIONS)

(THE DREAM)

Dream—kaleidoscope: a faded
broken glass revolves. Neither end nor beginning.
Mirrors always show a different pattern.
Every midnight a different story wounds me,
as the past trembles, is formed.

(NIGHT IN KOLOSZVÁR)

The statue of Matthias Corvinus circled by national flags.
Constantly pulled in one direction by the wind,
like dogs on a leash. Sniffing the air for fate.

Ha! There is no greater silence than that of mute
rail yards.
There is no path into silence. Only the nightmare of desire
finds a gap on the return journey.

Translated by Ottilie Mulzet

A GLOSS ON THE TEN COMMANDMENTS

1. I am the Lord your God, who brought you out of Egypt, out of the land of slavery.

I know who you are, Lord,
And I'm grateful to you.
But, sweet Lord above,
who else could I believe in,
when you're Yahweh,
Allah, Buddha, Isis,
Zeus, Jupiter, Ra,
Teotl, Scarabeus,
and Babba Mária,
Bull, Swan and the Bear;
when you're Pallas Athene,
Demeter, Hera, Charon,
The Ark of the Covenant, Nature
and Mind?
You're the Invisible and the
Only, constantly changing
your face and your place
for a new one—so every people in
every time can take in what you are,
can come to know you and find you.

You are a column of fire,
a footprint in the sand.

2. You shall have no other gods before me. You shall not make for yourself an image in the form of anything in heaven above or on the earth beneath or in the waters below.

So, no replacing your conceptual form
with a picture.

If All is One: and is also You—
then what is left of the world
to depict?
So, when I write, I should
keep your commandment—but how?

3. You shall not misuse the name of the Lord your God.

Anyone who badmouths you, Lord,
has no fear, but does have teeth of iron:
they fear no bolt from heaven . . .

4. Remember the Sabbath day by keeping it holy. Six days you shall labour and do all your work, but the seventh day is a sabbath to the Lord your God. On it you shall not do any work, neither you, nor your son or daughter, nor your male or female servant, nor your animals, nor any foreigner residing in your towns.

My Lord,
The servants, the animals, the labourers are resting.
Say 'Rest!' to the roaring elements,
say 'Halt!' to the avalanches,
to the lightning, the volcanoes, the bitter hail.
Tell hunger and tell thought
to take a break in the middle of a sentence,
tell the barking guns, and tell the
beggars, the children old before their time,

the epidemics and gleeful hatred,
tell the cramps, the fevers, the tumours,
that this is the sabbath, the day of rest—so stop!

For all of these let rest be blessed,
This is the actual Promised Land. Fix all
your eye can see in six days. Then on the seventh
just stand in this Earth, this other-world, and gaze.

5. Honour your father and your mother, so that you may live long in the land the Lord your God is giving you.

They're fallible, parents. Try to understand them,
but not in the hope of a long life—no!
Our old ones' tears are a concrete weight, their child's
disgrace. Regret will sweep in like a whirlwind later
and swallow us up.

6. You shall not kill.

Ah yes! The chief commandment.
I won't count the beetles, the hens or wasted days.
But who can tell what the naked flesh, the man–beast might
be induced to do by torture? Or terror? What can I promise?
I'm human, I just keep on saying, 'I will.'
And hands off even those who kill others—
that's what you're asking, right?
If that's a warning
that life is sacred, then let it be Untouchable,
let it be Unsnuffable, you, you almighty one!

7. You shall not commit adultery.

My Lord, my darling,
you do harp on about this. And I'm
not dealing with it.
Think of Lot, of Leda—
more come to mind, I imagine?

8. You shall not steal.

Fine, I'll try not to; not flowers, not books,
but not a title or an idea, even? Rebbe!
Our postmodern writing will die a death!

9. You shall not bear false witness against your neighbour.

False witness is like murder, really,
what spurts from some mouths, that sewage river,
could murder anyone.
People dripping with filthy words flick the dirt
onwards, hoping to blend in among the stained.

10. You shall not covet your neighbour's house. You shall not covet your neighbour's wife, or his male or female servant, his ox or donkey, or anything that belongs to your neighbour.

I covet no one else's goods.
But what if the body is another's, Lord?
And my body? Who does it belong to? Is it bad
for another to covet it? That won't mean it's lost to you,
Lord! But do not prohibit
the desires that pull us skywards either.
Nor wish us to be wily and tell lies.

You know what it says in *La Mandragola*: with time
'all that we have decays, only our morals improve.'

Translated by Anna Bentley

SENTIMENTAL RESEARCH

for Csaba Báthori

It is not only the newborn who have their dead.
It is not only the dead who leave someone behind.
It is not only the middle-aged, the young, who run among the living.
And not only on that road where others lie.
Not only they who murmur in words while alive.
Not only those who live, whom we cannot forget.
Not only the one who tenses his face forward.
Not only the old who grow blind into the future.
Not only the youth at the beginning of their past.
Not only the past, the dancer is embraced.
Not only the embrace dying in longer imagination.
Is our path guided only by persistent non-being?
We make our way between spectacle and perception.
We don't know, we don't know which is more circumspect:
To live for a while, or to keep watching until the end.
To know which older brother we are meant to replace.

Translated by Ottilie Mulzet

HOME

I came here among you.
But I never got there.
Beneath outspread arms,
stumbling, I went forward.
The outspread arms arrest me in flight.
The earth approaches, unattainable,
where I wish to go.
Where I'm straining with all
my strength, it backs away
into the fog, into a mistaken timetable.
This is where I wanted to come.
Even now, I'm walking on the road.
A few wings flung me here,
a friend's car took flight with me in it.
I left behind all my variegated
duties, escaped the obedient
anthill unto death.
I came here among you.
Ask and you shall receive.
The old courtyard drenched
in wine and sawdust. The arc lamp,
my still-tied bundle of clothes: resplendent.

Translated by Ottilie Mulzet

ZSUZSA RAKOVSZKY

(1950–)

THEY WERE BURNING DEAD LEAVES

They were burning dead leaves. Must oozed with scent,
    tar bubbled and blew.
The moonlight glow behind the thistle bent
    like a torn rainbow.

The street was a forest, night slid into the heart
    of deepest autumn.
A guilty music blew the house apart,
    with its fife and drum.

To have this again, just this, just the once more:
    I would sink below
autumnal earth and place my right hand in your
    hand like a shadow.

Translated by George Szirtes

INSOMNIA

The sun has ground down; but walls are throbbing
with activity: the chandelier radiates
wild spokes of light, pleats and wrinkles of glass
projected across the ceiling: insects throng
a central halo, wreathed about a single point,
their vast shadows billow through zones of light.

Windowpane: a charcoal room swims through grey water.
Light's dim double sways, a reduced incandescence,
flat black forms float through the mist-like mourners
of something left over, long dead. Light irritates,
sheathing my flesh in nylon, sheer, sticky with
perspiration; it melts and dazzles like boiled sweets.

The dial's luminous: I daren't go to sleep.
A dead woman lurks in the precincts of my dream:
she is cowering in her usual place on the divan,
or preparing to leave: she fiddles with her
knitted skirt which sizzles and clings to her stocking.
She paints her mouth, applies a pencil to her brow,

searches for her book, or for knitting needles in
a basket. I avoid her glance: she mustn't know . . .
by dawn she will have become a piece of paper tumbled
by the wind, an empty dress. She comes time and again

whenever I drift into broken sleep, from which
time and again I'm woken by lightning: her blinding
jagged profile, leaning against a phosphor-bright sky.

Translated by George Szirtes

FROM THE DUTCH SCHOOL

Groceries and herring on a table, or
a deck of cards scattered round dimpled glass.
In a chilly blue-green dusk, huge wagons ford
a stream, bearing an inferior class
of cabbage. Cellar stairs grow intimate,
winking under rain. A hand lifts a torch:
its faint effulgence picks away at night
unpeeling ivy and a corbelled porch.
By isolating them, the picture frame
draws out the sheer assertiveness of things,
a simultaneity in which herrings
cabbages and lit torches all proclaim
their *are* and *were*. But beyond such ebb and flow
lies time's third option: *not-here-not-I. No-go.*

Translated by George Szirtes

DECLINE AND FALL

At last they will disappear, finally just go,
those cinemas and cigarettes named after terms
derived from military history or constitutional law.
The waterworks, machine-tool factories, firms
producing matchboxes that advise you to pursue
a prudent lifestyle, they will vanish too.
Local branches of the catering industry,
chipped teacups, tubular plastic barstools made for
short legs, flat drinks in bottles whose labels sport
sun discs and oranges as if the real sun had bleached
them both, tables with marble effects and sticky
tops. They'll survive a while, persist like rime
in the coldest microclimate, in random patches,
but when they do eventually go it won't be time
but earth which swallows them, they will flake off
and soak away: anniversaries, occasions of formal
mourning, ersatz occasions that pass for normal:
Mother's Day, Women's Day, Children's Day, Sports Day,
each with its posters scrubbed, peeling away
to reveal a flowering branch or dove, or a block of
numbers pasted across a girl's virginal face,
(as if atoning for a Playboy playmate's vast
over-thrusting bunny bosom pressing against lace),

all these will fade away, as will the products
of the Totalitarian-Classical, filthy terminals
and waiting rooms, provincial culture halls
with monstrous frescoes and mosaics docked
of odd teeth, showing humanity gathered
in full-throated choirs, celebrating harvests,
or the manufacture of ball bearings, breasts
heaving in joy at the redemption of leisure
by culture. Not everything has weathered
so well: where are the experiments with white mice
or ferro-concrete? Burst like a balloon,
a thousand pieces exploding in one vast bloom,
or stretching, shrivelling, curling in long flames
resembling, if in nothing else but this,
a contemporary Rome or Babylon's nemesis.

My mass-produced mirror, my pot of jelloid face cream,
my little brown jugs, will not grace a museum,
provide educational outings for family Sundays,
nor will my remains be preserved in an airtight case
or my colour-rinsed curls and protruding eyes
be twisted into a sheath—my speaking likeness
will not be hung on the wall to oversee the moral
welfare of a new generation; indeed, of the wall,
a prefab component of my industrial highrise,
of that whole moon-grey incubator where each block
rots faster than the inner city's overblown baroque,
not a jot will remain. A few turn-of-the-century
public buildings, like slices of elephantine
wedding cake, blackened and growing green,
might yet survive, but their bills designed
for the propagation of an ornamental diction
and their six-foot streamers will have declined

and faded, their threadbare carpets rotted
to an ultimate state of dereliction,
and dehydrating yellow leaves of potted
palms perished in civic halls where council
employees, women in business suits, fill
forms, harangue, register marriages,
and rooms where we presented ourselves, signed up
for birth, death or divorce perhaps survive
preserved in memory's indifferent syrup
only while we who lived them are ourselves alive.

Translated by George Szirtes

OLD WOMEN OF MY CHILDHOOD

What else was there? The cocktail cabinet with pillar
base and marble top of raw-liver colour.
Cups thinning in light to a grey mist, a few
back numbers of a magazine called *New*
Age, silhouettes of greyhounds in an oval frame,
a souvenir glass, engraved with the name
of a German town. Their mode of being was curious:
imagine a cuckoo clock or ten-piece dinner service
salvaged for one's sole convenience from a wreck
and cast on a deserted beach among the bladderwrack
twixt goats and palm trees. Why furnish a room
with two tall facing mirrors? To reflect the gloom
of an unlit damp apartment, with neither kids nor maid?
Who'd use silver spoons for gruel, or provide
a pair of sugar tongs for a grain of rationed
sugar? What hope obliged them to preserve old-fashioned
gowns in the purgatory of the laundry chest?
Did they imagine themselves elegantly dressed
on promenades in fashionable parks, wearing one of those?
When did they realize that earnest suitors would not propose
to me in country residences while under the spell
of my dazzling rendition of *Für Elise*? Who can tell
what delusions they laboured under, the poor fools,
firmly convinced that fate would observe minimal rules
of etiquette, or how they contrived to maintain

their innocent beliefs. One might explain
away a dose of sickness or penury . . . but this?
Alice, grey-haired, meanders in a mist
of manners, still wearing her lacquered shoes;
having no clock-sense she's likely to confuse
the times of day; her dreams are like stiff dough.
(Better, perhaps, a dream world that you know
than a half-cock universe beyond control.)
Meanwhile the clocks chime on and hours unroll
as if time still existed and was somehow theirs
bringing a green-white froth of roseblight to squares
never referred to by new official names,
or twisting snow into apparitional white flames
to crown a bronze lion's monumental mane or shroud
the transmitting tower that sends time-signals out.
For one last time the broken blinds will clatter down,
patches on walls grow expansive, blotches of brown
skin on hands wear through, cigarette-paper-thin,
and watering eyes sink ever deeper in
a hutch of soft crushed bags. What else is there?
Only an over-exposed photograph, a white spectre
or candleflame in the foreground: outside, it might
be a winter evening, inside: electric light,
a festive tablecloth's sharp crease intrudes
into the picture and a fogged mirror broods
in circles. In clots of shadows which probably
dominate the background one might be able to see
among barely discernible patches, a faint outline
sufficient (with a little imagination) to define
a chin, shoulder or an unknown hand whose grey
boundaries too are finally washed away.

Translated by George Szirtes

JOURNEY BACK IN TIME

The American hypnotherapist Bruce Goldberg and his followers employ hypnosis to lead their patients back to their earlier lives, thus discovering the causes of their current problems.

As a copper ring, I was tossed into the fire.
A blinded cat, the mop bucket was my fate.
When king, I was remanded to the executioner.
I was a belt buckle, earth-buried for five millennia.

With crooked arms, with goitrous neck, I crouched,
in clouds of flies, next to a mud-stained river.
I baked flatbread on stone, indifferent, while
hundreds of dead floated past on sun-scorched waters.

I was an old woman too, dawdling all day
in my nightshirt, telling my grievances to the wall.
When I went out to get matches from the shop,
robbers stole half my peppers and my yellowed slip.

I drowned in the tub of a burning house.
I went to battle, and left behind my leg.
I wilted in my despotic mother's shadow.
In a peasant courtyard's dust, I was devoured by pigs.

I penetrated into ever thicker darkness.
Falling to the very edge of time—
as if plunging from a train at night, I saw nothing, only
diffused figures looming, but even there, I searched

for some originating goal, cause, or crime—but in the end
there was nothing, just some kind of wall.
And beyond that, only void, blue emptiness
with its slowly dying stars.

Translated by Ottilie Mulzet

PHANTOMS

There is no past tense. The past isn't even past.
We preserve it, just as the lakebed's silt
harbours the forest's pollen, long ago
burnt down to ash. That which was never reaches an end:
it ceases, and yet cannot cease at all.
Like the wasp trapped in the raspberry jam
no telling where that buzzing sound comes from,
or the crackling of a distant radio station
filtering into the gap between two words,
until some embankment is broken,
the fabric of the present finally gives way.
As when, taking pictures of empty streets,
camera loaded with ultrasensitive film,
snow-patched wheatfields, wind-rippled puddles—
then, in the developing tray, you're shocked
to see, marching across the fields
soldiers wearing strange uniforms . . .
There are refugees too: in trucks, on foot,
They're dragging heavy luggage, push
baby carriages piled high; some in tattered clothes,
an endless line—but in the road's dust,
in the vineyard mud, no footprints are left behind . . .

Or another time: on your way home,
climbing out from under your broken-down car
onto the muddy road as night quickly descends:

in jagged tire tracks, water glints
reflects the dark sky, the cheap bathtub
a mere faint patch; just beyond, a baby carriage
smashed onto tree roots,
then the moon, like a helium-filled balloon,
rises above bare twigs: in its light you see
tanks turning out from behind a hill,
a driver's face clearly visible, headed towards you,
you think: obviously, someone is making a film,
you venture one step forward: suddenly, a blast,
flames, another detonation, body burnt to char,
as if events of time past could not bear to keep spinning
away, and so can only repeat,
like a stuck gramophone record, into the wounded air . . .

Or you're a security guard on your midnight shift,
pocket torch searching weedy, empty lots:
here, where the old houses once stood
office buildings, parking lots planned to be built,
the beam of light excavates, from the night-time ground
brick piles, minor puddles, shovels cracked in half,
chalk-covered grasses—then you freeze in your tracks:
in the darkness there only looms
the cement mixer's stout outline; yet a crowd
is thronging there, jostling and shrill:
feet stamping, roast meat hissing, ringing of church bells,
children's sharp cries, chorales laconically sung,
nursery rhymes flitter above the barren ground,
drunken boasts drowned out by shrieking laughter—
just as warmth seeps from the walls of night,
so does there evaporate from the earth
the joy and suffering of absorbed sunken lives.

Or one evening you dash out, having forgot
the laundry outside: in the gentle breeze
the headless ghosts, swaggering, you see
them taking turns as they swing on the laundry line,
in the space between cellar door and garden wall,
a window pane lights up: a large yellow square
thrown across the dark grass of the yard,
the window sash shadow dividing it in four—
this yard has been the same for ten, for forty years,
and suddenly you feel: when you go back inside
to the deserted, empty room, you'll find
commotion, loud laughter, every light ablaze,
long-broken chalices brimming with red wine—
or just one person in their customary chair,
beyond the lamplight's circle, as they explain:
'I'm back: the full moon, or the magnet of your pain
convulsed the traces of my space-wandering being
into one body—so that I, who before
spoke of gas bills, faucets that leaked,
can say what I never said, and you too
tell me what you never told, while I still lived.'

Translated by Ottilie Mulzet

TRIPTYCH

1

Like the souls of the damned, or colicky infants,
cats are squalling in the moonless dark.
Five or so silent shades sit around,
awaiting their fate. Eyes like glass shards

as if from a hellish tunnel,
the headlights of an approaching train
from depths beyond time. From the latticed kitchen window,
from a dilapidated radio, the voice of a man

oozes onto the yard's tangled grass:
'to die . . . only for you . . . just a single kiss . . .'
While inside, a bath-robed woman mutters into her wine
about her husband and that wretched whore . . .

2

Light burns through the soda glass,
its soul splashes in the cup, a hissing arc.
A fly alights on the devil's tongue, hanging
from the lamp—black spot in the honey-hued pulp.

The girl isn't watching her usual programme tonight
but besieges mushy male advantage with a woman's rage—
thinking instead how she yanked back into place
her bicycle, damaged by the rain,

the man in the T-shirt, face freckled and burned,
his bulky hands pressed between his knees—
hoarse whispers, hardly heard
above blaring dance music. Behind the booths and the swings

the open field shudders blackly, undulates
in the sinking sun's chilly, golden rays.
As if the world were but a faint memory
of one moment's agitation, incandescent, filled with dread...

3

The bride is weeping in her white slip:
wants no wedding now, the iron scorched her dress ...
Relatives, copper-skinned from kitchen steam,
bandy-legged, tight-permed women tell her: hush.

Two children seated on chairs piled high with pillows,
we gaze with enchanted horror into the broth:
a pale rooster's head floats there, eyes closed.
Later on, starting awake from our dreams

we listen to thudding sounds, to harsh laughter
from beneath our shared quilt in the children's room.
Above are trembling stars, below are poultry droppings,
blackberries splattered in the dust of the yard.

Translated by Ottilie Mulzet

SONG ABOUT TIME

A comb buried in the ground, a wristwatch sunk in water,
a bird cadaver lying in the snow . . .
A Christmas card one century old
in the drawer that was hit by a bomb.
A bundle of pictures of those who are nowhere,
standing by the shore, leaning over a child,
its dark hair flutters in the summer wind.
Shards beneath the ruins of a house
long ago burnt in the fire of time.

The wan-lit pocket torch strains
to save something, anything from the night.
To blaze the nothing into borrowed existence.
To make, in a broken piece of mirror,
the past's extinguished decades glint.
As the rock is covered by foam,
as the ripple disperses in soundless water—
in the end only unwrinkled nonexistence remains,
as if there'd never been anything at all.

Translated by Ottilie Mulzet

IN AN ALPHA STATE

The house is scruffy, with a cat piss smell.
Windows gaze onto a darkened street.
Twilight-moss covers the walls,
the roof entreats the fading sun not to leave.
Inside, a chandelier weaves its skeins of light,
at the end of eight arms, eight gleaming spheres.
As guests arrive, they leave their coats outside,
just as they do with their cares:

The insurance company won't reimburse B.,
C.'s main contractor is committing fraud,
while D. tries to sell organic groceries
on the web. On expired ketchup bottles,
G. glues new labels. Behind their eyes
rustles a secretive garden. On the crowns of their heads
the chakras open, through their bodies
floods the Universe's energy.

The vast shades of four heads cast on the ceiling,
on the platter, herbal tea and multigrain bread.
They stare into a candle, flickering,
eyes foggy, the tips of their fingers meet
as they drift across the layers of their souls,
into depths where space and time catch
flame, are extinguished—then they recount
what they saw, as each returns.

'What did you see? I saw a lake
of clear blue, at its centre, a rose floating.
In the blazing sun, I cut through a field,
it was noon, bluebells were swaying.
Then I stepped across heavy stone gates,
before me there appeared dour faces of stone,
they perspired shadowless, below in the depths,
beneath the blood-coloured cave moon.'

'There was a room—the salty sea scent
drifted in through the window. A pendulum clock
struck midnight. It was foggy and dark,
candles flickered, draughts blew, as we sat,
awaiting a ship that never came. The sun rose,
snow fell, scattered with some drops of blood.
The narrow walls beat back the rumbling of God,
as we waited, tossed in the cold billows of fate.'

'A red brick wall in the noonday sun,
before it, crocuses in the narrow front
garden. Green grass of summer rain.
A house where I was expected—and was late.
But where was I, and was I still myself?
Beneath rain-battered rocks, my body was naught
but empty bones. I heard background music:
roaring, God besieged the shore.'

Now three pairs of eyes are looking at D.:
they know he searches for the secret of Life.
They see as his hands' moon-shaped nails
hesitate in the air for a moment.
As if he were wading onto the shore
from the waters of dreams, in stone-heavy clothes,
as if he were a statue made to come alive,
D. looks around, slowly his tongue begins to turn:

'I saw a city which exists in no land.
Between earth and sky: the meeting place,
lengthwise, of two points. There was neither sun nor moon,
no season ever passed, no time of day.
Into the narrow intervals, yellowish fog loomed,
nothing could be seen beyond the window frames.
Like a giant amoeba's body, the fog swallowed all,
began to eat away at the borders of all things:

'no more difference between the living and the dead,
between dark and light, between good and bad.
I saw a man breastfeeding a snake,
I saw a woman swear allegiance
to a microwave. My own mother became
a fire hydrant. Behind the dense fog
endless battles raged, houses fell to rubble,
the main bus station swept away by floods,
boats sunken in flame-devoured water.
Yet none of this was real in any way.

'An angel came along and said: "This is heaven.
Or hell. Anyway, it makes no difference.
Where substance no longer exists,
the meaning of words also vanish.
This is not space, but its mere recollection.
These are not people, only phantoms.
Just like yourself—don't nurture delusions!
You don't exist, it's only an illusion!"
And so I wept, and weeping, began to search
for a sensation, some solid point in space,
but found nothing—for all was constant change.

How good that I returned here among
you—from this place I cannot name!'

Translated by Ottilie Mulzet

STAR

A star is burning behind my closed eyes,
in the unconscious' darkened borderlands,
everything else covered over by fog—
that was the beginning; so it shall remain.

A fixed star above the running years.
In the tapestry of facts, a needle's perforation.
And beyond these ceaselessly changing images,
only the self—a shard of God, or a friar's lantern?

A phantom light, luring us, frenzied,
to its swamp? A never-slumbering pilot flare,
the reflections of two facing mirrors?

The imagined world's glitter, in dead clay stored?
Into that fog, bereft of space or time,
o Star, will you guide me to the Grey Port?

Translated by Ottilie Mulzet

AUTUMN

The golden eye of a single daisy—
emblem of the memory of a garden.
Apricot moon: the spirit of August
haunts between two sumac tree branches. Within,

the summer things descend
into their wooden trunks, their graves. Two moths quiver,
flying from the cabinet-night. In your hands,
from September chestnuts, small carved figures emerge.

Electric light, smoke: it is autumn now. But still
the autumn of immortal beginnings—the year
a whirling snail in the hands of gods.

And I, with immortal eyes, look upon the moon
between two shutters, midnight's navel
swelling with the future in the pregnant-death sky.

Translated by Ottilie Mulzet

FORTEPAN: FOREST

Houses on only one side of the street.
No longer the city, but not yet forest.
Dilapidated villas, one named 'Lilla', perhaps
the embodied dream of a former
brewer or malt factory owner, roses ramble
on the northern wall with its small round tower,
a veranda where, at noon, a brief-lived shadow
come to meet the walnut tree's dark foliage.
Tea time, fallen apples, children's toys left
outside: a map with memory replete,
made by spirits, delineating the garden
before it's overgrown by ragweed.

But the woodbine-swathed iron
lances suddenly come to an end.
Space narrows to tapered paths
between tree stumps and benches, where
the forest begins: pale green looms,
a spring pours out spume onto pipe of rusted iron;
no blue trail markings along this route,
only mossy tree trunks designate the North.
Light-patches quiver on grass, atop bushes,
then a steep path leading up
to the lookout named for an erstwhile president
of a choral society or a hiking club,

then across the darkened cells,
through echoing staircases of iron,
onto the balcony, where squadrons of pines
extend, leafy crowns' wind-tossed sea.

Beyond there are mountains, and more mountains beyond,
behind which lies what can't be thought:
for behind the horizon are the exiled gods
still living as pine trees, or in brambleberry form.
Where no footpath has ever traversed
waist-high grassy undergrowth,
and no human eye has ever glimpsed
the blackthorn that resides within the flower,
where Existence has thrown off its disguise,
a fallen leaf drifts in a silken water pond.
We won't get that far today, although
it seems to me that was our plan,
but it's autumn, and already growing dark,
and no time left—because now there's an end
to dusk, its slowly fading signal lights,
in this humid obscurity, beneath the trees' damp,
our footprints washed away by torrenting rains.

Translated by Ottilie Mulzet

FINAL DAYS

I've put in forty years
in this dusty province at the end of the world,
where nothing ever happens. For forty years,
I've been gazing at the mountains'
barren contours, the mud-hued river,
these few wretched streets,
mud-brick and wooden houses,
(in the summer suffocated by dust,
in the winter, cut off the world by snow),
and those few provincial villas up on the hill,
where the tart grapes are grown,
acrid, miserly vines in a cloudy terrain
(the wine pressed from them
is usually undrinkable). The Capitol
attempts to mimic a city: in its centre
stands the hulking triad: Jupiter, Hera and Minerva,
the rough, slipshod chisel lines
testify to a third-rank master
(not only that, Minerva's nose is broken off!)
But never mind: no one respects them
anymore anyway, just like
Mithras and all those other gods
with unremarkable epithets, their origins
obscure. In times of trouble, illness,
and freezing rain, we dash beneath their wings,

panicked and unbelieving, but as soon as the sun comes out,
we forget them. They live on, at the very most, as mere names,
the object of trite similes
in easy-flowing poesy—even here,
at the end of the world, such verses are composed
by a few embittered and disgraced
functionaries, decommissioned soldiers,
or dabbling exiled orators,
seeking to dispel an empty evening's tedium.

In the meantime, beyond the river,
eyes like hungry wolves' eyes,
thousands of eyes, tens of thousands of eyes,
flash dangerously, observing us
from the oak forest's fog, where in sacred groves,
in the deep darkness of trees, in brooks,
the gods live, and above the barren cliffs
there floats a godly face of pure gold: the moon.
Where every man is a warrior, and every child,
as soon as it can walk, with broken
branch, with dry stalks, practises the art of fencing:
the women dressed in rough cloth,
eternally breastfeeding, struggling to light fires,
not knowing the ruses of love which
can strike desire from revulsion,
because even revulsion is unknown to them,
their life ruled by bleak
virtue, an excess of blind faith.

At times I try to see us
with their eyes, with the merciless
discernment of jealousy, loathing
and contempt, or with that impassive
hunter's glance, searching, from obscurity,

to glean the habits of its prey:
we are pitiful beings, no doubt!
Our sense of danger dulled, our bodies
bloated from inaction, from all
the meat and exotic spices.
Boredom, anxiety and bad digestion
bleaches our skin to pale yellow-grey—
we are grey like phantoms,
pale, like spirits of the dead,
because that is what we are:
the moving, eating, copulating dead!
Like shadows, we wander in a shadow-world,
where the source of life has become parched,
our souls empty, our minds grinding away at nothing,
our destruction merited long ago!

Many times, if at night
I am pacing, sleepless, and I watch the water
as it shines emptily, the stars' black mirror,
I see the approaching shadows
of the boats, shadows
of people, I see the rhythmic movement
of their soundless oars, I hear the silence
of the last minutes, before the howling
breaks out, making the walls violently tremble:
the arrows hissing, broken bones
splitting and cracking, skulls smashed in,
the howling of the flames as they devour
the wood and mud bricks, the assembled
detritus of my life. When I think about it,
I see all that surrounds me now,
this dismal view, its endless tedium, the mud brick
walls, Minerva's broken-off nose,

as if they were already mere memories,
memories growing pallid, memories of what
shall soon be dust and ashes.

And then every object, of which I am
so weary, at once begins to shine with saturated,
incandescent light, as objects
become luminous only before nightfall,
and suddenly I am seized with such tenderness,
such a blind outpouring of love,
that its mere fragment,
a mere morsel would be sufficient,
—if it were not too late, if there still were time—
for me to save, and to protect, at any cost,
all this and myself.

Translated by Ottilie Mulzet

FACE

REMBRANDT: PORTRAIT OF AECHJE CLAEDR

I know that face from somewhere:
one hundred years ago, or this afternoon,
I saw her picking apples at the market
in sparse autumn light, cat underfoot,
the two vertical pleats engraved above

her nose, chiselled by a whole life's
worry and cares: behind her old, startled eyes
all of that life's light and shadow:
cooking, wash days, ill-intentioned folk,
meagre harvests, infants with running bowels,

tranquil Sundays spent with the tapestry needle,
kittens, in buckets of water drowned,
the May altar decorations for the Blessed Mother,
winds blowing, hail falling, heat, light, and frost,
children departing for distant shores.

The white capelet, the bonnet with its veil—
This is a face that was never young.
It cannot be tied to any place or time,
when I was two years old, she held my hand.
Time makes other faces resemble itself,

and they too leave their handprints upon time.
There are those who polish their existence only once:
poets, popes, soldiers and kings
held up as an emblem for some city or land
while they themselves, as statues, keep existing,

their footprints remaining in the dust of that age . . .
But she comes to us in somewhat different guise,
not clinging to one land or century,
she has no immortal self-engraved in stone,
falling apart, then reassembled, a dark river's spume.

Translated by Ottilie Mulzet

DREAM

TIVADAR CSONTVÁRY KOSZTKA: BRIDGE AT MOSTAR

Something has happened here. There are no people
anywhere. Only sky and stone and water. The houses
drenched in the hard light of the summer sun.
Empty doorways. Empty window frames.

The trees seem to live, but the hill
has turned to stone, not even one leaf trembles,
as I myself wander here,
like a ghost. Did I die, or am I dreaming?

The shadow of the walls cast dark stripes
on the path's stones, burning in the heat.
It is noon. Motionless clouds in the sky.

It's as if I saw something moving
on the bridge . . . the water is still and does not flow,
I would run, but I myself cannot move.

Translated by Ottilie Mulzet

POLEMIC IN LIVING TIME (SELECTIONS)

A.:

Light-filled weeks, the holiday draws close,
to arise at dawn when it's still dark,
on the way to Rorate mass, shivering in a greatcoat,
up to my knees in snow, only half awake . . .

I remember once a midnight candlelight procession,
It was May, the month of Mary, lilacs' effervescence,
another world lay above our daily lives,
behind our night another night, transcendent.

Like coming into a well-lit, heated room
from outside, from the wind and the cold,
that is how we look back upon that secure age
as if ghosts, trapped outside of existence.

Earthly water does not quench the soul's thirst,
our home is not located here in space and time.
Perhaps the age will save us from worse tortures,
but in the sandy desert, the soul grows parched.

B.:

The soul grows thirsty, but always for something else
than what it has: for Byzantium's golden fire,
when tranquil, it yearns for wild enchantment,
at home it yearns to leave, in peacetime yearns for blood...

Like a train always shuttling between two end points,
with hope only in between, at the border of two worlds.
There's no middle path, fidelity ties your hands,
you can be free, but only at the price of Self.

You may choose another continent on which to reside,
another epoch, or another star,
but you won't find abatement for your thirst:
the measure of this world wasn't made for our souls.

A.:

Warm clothes stored among mothballs for the winter.
Thyme and rosemary growing in planters.
Next to the stove, the umpteenth generation of dogs,
while time expands in the furniture, the walls ...

The series of generations intertwined,
although cataclysms may rupture the line,
but then between two rocks, a random seed is tossed,
spurting up in our basement, a dark underground stream.

The dead reside with us, invisibly,
their hands' spirit-print upon the windows and the doors.
Past torments and joys circulate in the walls,
what once was their life, we carry forward.

Translated by Ottilie Mulzet

GNOSTIC

How I ended up here on this earth,
I don't recall, or even where I was born.
For years now, weighty dreams enthralled me,
because I live here, I have eaten of their food.

The soul yearns to be free, but in the end
dead material yanks it back to itself.
The splendour of an immaculate feeling,
light with no source, a smile with no mouth,

the soul sinks through the circles of sky,
as the unfamiliar desires cling,
slowly growing dark, it sees itself
in material's half-obscure mirror

where everything that is soul appears as corporal,
in Creation's developing bath:
from pain will be earth, from desire will be air,
delight births fire, shame begets mud.

The lost soul descends ever lower,
fading, deteriorating in time,
its essence barely ignites a flame,
the spark inherent in the linden tree, the stone,

but trapped inside its living prison
by the body—the blind guard who betrays,
until the prison door is flung open by death
and it soars, casting away existence's weight.

Translated by Ottilie Mulzet

KRISZTINA TÓTH

(1967–)

SHADOWGRASS

I set about to put everything in order:
to mow the lawn, but first I had
to disentangle the twenty-five metres
of extension cord.
One end I tied to an arbour vitae
(oh, how the route passes from soul to soul)
with another (there were at least four).
I headed back to the house.
Evening closed in around me and I gave up.
Stay—I stood there—stay as it is,
let it grow ever further and scatter forth,
growing onto the sky, may the shadowgrass
scatter forth its seeds,
which I myself have cast.

Translated by Ottilie Mulzet

NEW YEAR'S EVE

So here's another year that I've sent packing.
It's leaving right now, all dressed up as snow.
I know you exist, that it is you I'm lacking
and that's OK since you're out there, I know,

in some imaginable solid place
or pretty close, lost to a different night,
though when I look there searching for your face
they're strangers all, and you're nowhere in sight,

and even I, when I unpack my bag
seem to be carrying other people's stuff:
handkerchiefs, keys, soaked identity tag,
would you know me by such things, is that enough?

Could you tell me by my shoes, the coat I wear?
In cloakrooms could you recognise the one
I carried and confidently declare
that it was mine before I put it on?

I see this very room as in a mirror:
as familiar yet strange, a spacious den,
a life I'd entered by some kind of error,
a night I should sleep off and start again

after a millennium of heavy sleep.
Let me forget you, may you sink so deep
that when they ask me for my name, may I
not answer with your name when I reply.

Translated by George Szirtes

THE MOUSE

for Zsuzsa Beney

In the book of the poet who lives no more,
next to a verse where he writes of a woman,
(she too lives no more) like a dandelion
is preserved the pawprint of my cat:

stealthily creeping there, for the crack
between the pages was always exciting,
waiting for the mouse at once to come out,
(the cat too has long since gone missing)

and truly in the depths of the paper's secret
tunnel, something flutters, incessant—
something we have left between the leaves:
the accidental there impressed.

Translated by Ottilie Mulzet

CLOTHES

In the stagnant pools dead water
You shadow-pendulum breeze
The clatter of swings in Lichthof
A child drying off

All at once everything speaking
Splashing in the wash
Dead time flows on
From the clothes, the word

Translated by Ottilie Mulzet

MACHINE VOICE

For beyond the beyond of your earthly time
it hadn't been you for so long, for I saw you, I saw you
a dead person spoke on your answering machine
still l could not stop
calling you back, to call you back again

on your way for so long already and you could not stop
nor body nor voice, only a form going away
anyone could have spoken, you didn't turn around
still I couldn't stop
calling you back, to call you back again

nor body nor voice, only a form going away
beyond the beyond of your earthly time
I called out to you once in vain
a dead person spoke on your answering machine
still I could not stop

calling you back, to call you back again
anyone could have spoken, you didn't turn around
for beyond the beyond of your earthly time
on your way for so long already and you could not stop
I called, called out to you in vain

Translated by Ottilie Mulzet

EAST EUROPE TRIPTYCH

I.

The loudspeaker calls out our names
and we jump up. Our names are
misspelled and mispronounced,
but we smile graciously.
We take the soap from the hotel,
and arrive too early at the station.
With heavy suitcases, in baggy trousers,
everywhere one of our compatriots loitering.
The trains go with us in the wrong directions,
and if we pay, the small change rolls everywhere.

At our borders we're afraid, and beyond that
we get lost, but recognize each other.
We know the other side of the world,
the sweat-drenched clothes beneath the coat.
Below us stands the escalator, the handle
of the shopping bag filled to bursting rips, and when
we leave, the alarm goes off.
Beneath our skin, like a radiating jewel,
is the microchip of a guilty conscience.

II.

I know where you live, I know that city well.
I know that black rainfall.
Your mother used to sunbathe on the roof,
in the summer you swam in the quarry lake.
I know that man, his legs amputated,
who lives in the entranceway.
I know that country, I know
its trains, its cries, its chlorine skies,
its acid rains, its lingering snowfalls,
its pale overly swaddled infants.

I know where you live. No matter where it is,
if you think of home, the road bordered
with the stumps of acacia trees
haunts you in your dreams.
During the feast, when they drag in
the tree, like a too-heavy dead man, grabbing it by the foot,
you stop and look as it is trundled towards the others.
I know what you see: the dishevelled heap of human bodies,
on every one of their extended yellow hands
a forgotten jewel: plundered
blue and gold Christmas-candy wrappers.

III.

My name is Alina Moldova.
I come from Eastern Europe,
I am 170 centimetres in height,
my life expectancy is 56 years.
I have amalgam fillings in my teeth,
in my heart I carry an inherited dread.
When I speak English, no one understands me,

when I speak French, no one understands me,
It is only the language of fear
that I speak without an accent.

My name is Alina Moldova.
My heart valves are an unmanned rail crossing,
poisons circulate within my veins,
my life expectancy is 56 years.
I support my ten-year-old son,
I get hold of some flour, step onto moving trains.
You can hit me, you can shake me,
but my earrings only jangle a little,
like a loosened part
in a motor still running.

Translated by Ottilie Mulzet

SLEEPER

Where have you been, Sleeper, tell us about the server
that transmits such shaky images across the foggy water,
were you a seagull, did the precarious dream of
clinging to a mast seek you on some guano-covered cliff,
and were you dizzy, as you never had been before
so you saw how it was no use, that earth was no more
than the slippery minute, a cloakroom of woods and bodies,
a roar in a colonnade you must cross fully awake however unsteady
the way, could you see it as from above, a gorge compounded
of a single cry, tell us, Sleeper, what is it that is suspended
above the mountain, under the breathing sky and how light moves
through the huge pink cloud of the lungs, how the cuts and grooves
of the mouth gurgle with foam and how the stalactite
of the uvula sparkles in the dripping valley of the throat,
and further still what images are etched by salt, lime and ice,
how earth is just a folded map, how God stares into the pit of the eye,
tell us what water says and what is slopping in the ranks of waves,
what are the creatures buzzing, and does it hurt when they weave
and change shape, when naked gooseflesh under fur gone cold
and dropped feathers throbs, screams, quivers and is called
by name, where have you been Sleeper, recount your flimsy,
whirlpool dreams of oil-slicked seas and seventeen tons of greasy
hair, tell us of wounds still smoking on earth scarred with fire,

give us aerial views of bridges like white stitches and of tight
twists of fate, the intricate fingerprints of winding highways
on a well-thumbed world as you swim past the breakwater of estates,
show us, Sleeper, the shadow island of fishes and large ships
and how the dead set out in search of other forms of life for fellowship,
how the tides of the sky rock the buoys of the stars, how they all fall away,
how vapour is ground down to breath, and how the blue light sways
on creaking chains and twilight, then swims on, its heavy metal seeping
into mud, and tell us of the corridors you passed through while sleeping,
how many vast spaces you crossed, and how the secret moment becomes
a door and what it's like to step into such cold, unlit fiefdoms,
does anything remain, do you recall the foam of your life, think back,
do you carry your fate like the slow flow of the corpse in a sack,
does the noisy past roll past you on its carpet in your occasional presence
or are you talking to the ocean through a thousand years of silence,
repeating what the radar of your brief life enabled you to witness
tell us little pulse box, will the soul sink into depths above us
or will it spin and billow like a bladder of light, understanding nothing,
blind, transparent, a never decomposing, murderous thing,
an empty flask of pills, doomed to roam the sky's thin covering?

Translated by George Szirtes

TYRANNOSAURUS REX

I remember nothing of Maribor,
nothing that I should remember.
All I know I have learnt from others:
I don't remember those three days.

I remember nothing of Ljubljana either
only that you promised you would come.
Ljubljana is just a hotel to me.
Ljubljana means simply: you're not there.

I remember nothing of the mountains
but everyone waiting on the bus for me.
I was busily counting up my cash
because I had spotted a dinosaur backpack.

I bought it for my son but had no room for it.
I ran because the driver was sounding his horn.
For a whole week I carried that backpack
up and down Slovenian mountains.

Those who saw me will remember only
a woman, possibly Polish, maybe Hungarian,
who carried her luggage in a dinosaur backpack
and never once spoke to anyone that week.

It turned out, at the beginning of the term,
that dinosaur backpacks were immensely popular
though it should be said that, among backpacks,
Tyrannosaurus Rex was the rarest and the largest.

Emperor of lizards, insatiable carnivore,
you were not slow in gobbling up my days.
Somebody, one time, mentioned Ljubljana
and that the name derives from 'city of love'.

I waited for you a whole six million years
but only once did we speak to each other after.
Such deep dull hurt is doomed to meet its sad
demise, the way the dinosaurs met theirs.

Translated by George Szirtes

ANY COUNTRY IN THE WORLD

The pollen was swirling, the crematorium wasn't signposted,
the tin roof of the building with its corkscrew chimney
appeared at the end of the concrete path. I recognised it. Someone
was using a cell phone in the yard. The gate was wide open,
I said hello thinking I should leave but a man stopped me
so I asked the way to the office. If it's about your grandmother
you are just in time, he said, it's all ready to go.
I didn't dare ask him what exactly he meant.
In order for her to be legally cremated I had to produce her ID
proving that she was a citizen of Hungary and that she had died.
I put the papers on the table, a woman was fiddling with a typewriter,
the passport opened precisely on the middle fold like a window
in the airless room, on an official stamp declaring that the bearer
was entitled to travel to any country in the world.

It was a hall in any country of the world and I stood
in front of the grey monitor with its gentle hum
and gazed at my grandmother's face, made-up
as if for a journey while her body rolled down the rails,
and she still looked like herself, only her nose seemed
a little bit sharper, apart from which she looked like any dead person,
mottled with jaundice, her throat yellow, simply a body
now released from the prison of this world of vanities
as they slid her away, and suddenly I couldn't look
and is summoned hence to heaven, so they offered me

a seat, saying, do sit down if you would like to stay to the end,
but I had to go, to collect the children from school,
and they were pushing buttons and the electric hum
began, it was one forty-six. I don't believe in
the resurrection of the weather-beaten body.

In the turbine motor of summer, the sky was babbling dry rain,
I kept blinking, the warm wind still blowing outside,
stirring scratchy clouds, bearing them along, sweeping them
centrestage but it wasn't for her I was weeping,
we hadn't spoken in years, nor for her face, her hands nor
for my pale childhood, but the body, the body alone, just the body
because that's all there was, skin peeling, lilac fingernails, that's all,
because I am a hollow body and I can't bear not loving you,
because every country in the world is an abandoned body
without a home, because the body would never reach home,
and cars were sounding horns, a cyclist swerved round me
so the dust on the skin slowly settles on the heart,
two hours must have passed and I knew she was still burning
as I set off down a road behind the Auchan warehouse
to find the nearest local train.

Translated by George Szirtes

COLD WEATHER

When friends or neighbours call around I'm sure
to find something behind dad's wardrobe door
that fits them fine.

Item by item they leave with what survives
of him, of the same size, so many lives
waiting in line.

How many fathers bidding a last good bye?
He's there in everything they take or try.
How cold it is!

He's there, his back turned, in the evening light.
I meet him in the street and recognise him by sight,
each shadow his.

Translated by George Szirtes

TIME, TIME, TIME

At a relative's house, back in my childhood,
among the clumsy furniture, in the crowded flat
of a widowed forester wearing a flannel shirt,
there towered a vertical clock with a door
you could open. It was full of mechanical parts
that made it look mysterious yet pointless
like the empty dovecote in the courtyard
of a block where some of my school friends lived.
It's an upright clock, the adults earnestly told me
and since it had not worked for years, I felt
it must owe its dignity to its unmoving hands.
My parents wore wristwatches but never had the time
so I began to pine for a distant realm elsewhere
where I would eventually get to own
an upright clock of my own whose hands
could not be touched by anyone else

Don't hold us up, they demanded, whenever we set out.
One day I was bored. I was sitting on the floor,
leafing through a hunting manual, gazing
at images of wide-eyed rabbits and deer.
It's hard work holding up people. Years pass before
you learn to get inside and behind time's back.
I delay whatever I can in the shadows.
I drag dead time along, its feet tied closely together,

pulling it behind me like a sledge.
What is that string, they ask, and what's at the end of it?
What are you dangling over the horizon?
Nothing, I tell them. Other times they ask
who is actually doing the pulling.
It's me, I answer on such occasions,
me when I'm older.

Don't run out of time, they used to say to me,
or you won't get a degree, a house, or a child,
you'll miss the last bus, the love of your life,
you won't be a ballerina or a young mother
not even an old one, you can't simply run
through a crowd on bare feet the whole of your life,
just look at your feet, you are still wearing
those sandals from childhood, its straps are loose,
quickly now, hurry, catch up with the others!
I ran like a deer, like a rabbit, in different shoes,
in dream shoes, my eyes open wide,
my stomach retching, my ribs pounding,
always falling behind, always stumbling
towards a corner of the picture. When I looked up
it was dark already and my time was up.

Translated by George Szirtes

VATERA

I was looking for a doll, a small children's doll
to replace the old one my daughter had lost,
a doll as much like the first one as possible.
It would make her a present at Christmas.

I wrote that it should be a second-hand item
but one in perfect condition, hoping
that among so many I would find one exactly
like the first and dress it in new clothes.

But good heavens, how did this get here?
This is not what I ordered, this is no baby,
not this double-folded tortured creature,
but this was what the screen showed me.

I bid for it but was outbid by someone
who wanted a little girl with a terrified face,
a four-foot-three high silicone woman
wearing knee socks and sandals.

There was, said the advertisement, a choice
of three colours for hair and more for the eyes,
with three welcome accommodating slits,
womb length six inches, fluids provided.

The fluids were intended for cleaning.
Someone out there had already paid the price,
and it had been sent out, so it would have a daddy.
Packing discrete, delivered by messenger.

I would have liked to take the body away
so I could give it a decent burial
in the longish box provided, before
the ground froze hard in winter.

A cardboard coffin containing childhood.
I would have scraped some soil over it
so something within it should find rest at last,
but the price was too high. It was too much to pay.

There's always a face somewhere
that reminds us of another, a lost face,
but when I call to it, it sinks under the surface
and starts crying again whenever I look for it.

There's always some minor detail missing from it.
How often did I hear my father say, You're priceless.
God couldn't buy you from me. But where is he now,
dear God, and what is the price to be paid?

Translated by George Szirtes

DURATION

Everyone's gone, that's what it says on the paper,
it's the poor line I have been reciting as mantra.
It is not a good line. I shouldn't have written it.
There's a scratchy sound. The electric clock is a nuisance.
It's never silent here. A neighbour is shouting on her cell phone,
using unfamiliar terms that don't fit the poem.
Completion, duration, functioning business plan.
I am waiting for him to finish the conversation.
Down in the street he is arguing about time
with a phantom, how it can't go on like this.
If she gave up now I'd be doing the same,
talking about time, here in this poem.
I stand and lean from the window so I can see her.
There was a storm last night and the street is still wet.
There's a phrase in my head but it can't get out.
Something unexpected has blown the circuit.

On the path by the house there's a tall unidentifiable
plant growing from under the bushes.
I leave it there and return to the bad line
but now that I've noticed the plant the thought of it
bothers me. *Duration.* Another hour wasted,
what is the phrase, good heavens, where will this end,
I stand up and walk down to the car park
to explore the plant that is in the bushes.

There I discover a Mermaid Barbie with a crushed head
its mermaid tail stuck in the ground. It's as if it were
trying to tell me that it's under some kind of curse
that I should be lifting so it can get back in the water.
What is it doing here? It must be the storm
that has blown it away, or someone dropped it last night.
I am standing in the car park, bending over
as the mud-caked Barbie's eyes stare back at me.

And now what to do, what should I do now,
am I ever going to get some silence here?
Maybe someone is watching me from upstairs?
What has this strange moment to do with me?
Should I pull the thing out of the ground so it
sheds earth every night, because however often
we wash it, or wrap it in a tissue or leave it
on the radiator we'll only have to bin it in the end?
Or should I leave it here, so it might grow a little
each night like a scary, blonde, mutant carrot,
shaking its mountain of hair across our fervid future
as if in revenge, casting sand even on years to come,
when I will always have to see it in front of me,
pushing me forward and down inviting me to share her fate?
I stand there in my slippers, my coat open
and everyone's gone, like the line says, everyone's gone.

Translated by George Szirtes

SONG OF THE SECRET LIFE

My secret life is that of a cat sneaking between parked cars,
a shadow on a wall, a memory, its hem ripped apart,

My secret life is lived at the edge of your widening cornea, discreetly,
close the lids of your scratched eyes on me, close them completely,

My secret life is an echoing empty room in my head
where I leant from the window once and sang of blackness and dread.

My secret life is a ramshackle pigeon loft stinking of shit,
a pale frock in the sky into which death will eventually fit.

My secret life is a deep crack that runs down a living face,
a path under time where I no longer rage, a singular place.

My secret life is a station where a train thunders through it and then
nothing but silence, pitch darkness, while I count to ten.

My secret life consists of moments quickly scanned in,
a crumpled page from a lost notebook found in the bin

My secret life is a lacking, an utter mystery, a puzzle undone,
so you have to read all my fading faces as if they were one.

My secret life is landfill, yellow and overflowing,
the lusts of the body in movement, time spent coming and going.

My secret life is kept secret on purpose with doors I always lock,
where dreams come at dawn with their knuckles and loudly knock.

My secret life is this thing you see passing, you catch it neatly,
close the lids of your scratched eyes on me, close them completely,

My secret life is one I've invented, to survive it needs telling,
its lightbulbs burn in the house, in that far distant dwelling.

Translated by George Szirtes

OVEN GLOVE

Pale, pitiful palm,
washed-out oven glove,
belly crushed, wrinkled,
shrunk after long drying.

Bright mauve at the start,
now blotched and faded:
a wizened hand, its skin
patched with liver spots.

I wonder what you want, mother,
you wrinkled, blotchy hand.
There's just one of you, no pair.
You know there was always just one.

Too frail to embrace or to pick up,
I was a hot little saucepan,
sweat-pearled, feverish and steaming,
but you didn't reach out for me.

Perhaps I should throw it out.
I really should get round to it.
I shouldn't have bothered to wash it.
I don't even know what I hoped for.

After three solid hours
in boiling water, every last
patch of dark soaks away.
How many lives do you need?

What is the correct setting for this?
There are no settings, just the one
for this ever paler, singleton,
this glove, like a human hand.

Translated by George Szirtes

WHERE

Not there, on the tight bend of the paved highway,
where cars are occasionally prone to skidding,
chiefly in winter, though no one dies there,

not there where streets are greener and leafier
where lawns are mowed and there's a dog in the garden
and the head of the family gets home late at night,

nor there in front of the school where every morning
a man is waiting regular as clockwork,
nor inside the gates on the concrete playground,

nor in the neglected, dehydrated meadow
where a discarded dog-end hits the ground and glows
for a moment, it doesn't begin there

but at the edge of the forest, in rotting humus
where somebody once was buried alive,
that's where the poem begins.

Translated by George Szirtes

ANNA T. SZABÓ

(1972–)

'44, TIRESIAS

On the photo Blind Musician on the banks of the Danube, 1944, *by Károly Escher*

1

The world of the spirits has fallen asleep.

Blind fate shrieking, living wound.
God's beggar. What is he hoping for?

Here on the riverbank, leaning against the sidewall.
Where there is no law, only will.
He has no homeland, only betrayal.
Where no one sees him, only the Contax II.

With damned soul, useless,
I scream into vast infinity:
I am the world—everything that was, is,
and I feel them, and I remember them.

He doesn't see, doesn't hear who stands above him.
If it is a gun is aimed at him, or a camera.
He doesn't want to be alive. He is alive.
Shouting from rent throat.

2

The eye is white inside.
Black blood on the stone.

The water is flowing, the water reflecting,
mutely, like an angel who marvels at destruction,
because everything returns.

October, cold.
Who dares come here?
The wind rattles the leaves.
The flag on the machine-gun clatters.

Today at midnight, they emptied the hospitals. An old lady moaned under her breath the entire way.

Fire—

And yet the stone, as if it were our bones
And the wave, as if our blood that flows
By the Danube
Ruddy from scarlet blood
At last the sun—
how far can you retreat—

Fire—

He hears everything, he hears nothing.
He drags the bow.
So that the melody will pass through hearts
He drags the bow.
Along the Dniester's twisted course
a Hungarian unit retreats from its trench
He drags the bow.

Drag the bow, gipsy, you drank away your fee.
He drags the bow.

Fire—

Oh, does my home still exist?
His father is at the front. His son at the front.
He too is at the front. He has no home.
Home he does not have.
Does not have.

It's burning, brothers, burning,
smoke and wreckage,
they just stand there, looking—
Fire—

Murderous brother—
I fell next to him—
There are no civilians.

3

This train is about to depart,
the locomotive festooned, wreathed
like cemeteries, gravestones reeling—
if I have no homeland

Into the cattle cars.
The passers-by spit.

Into the cattle cars as well, the flower-wreathed soldiers.
The passers-by salute.

Fire—

They yank out the dead from among the sleeping.

Dawn, mass grave.
They have no names.
No one knows where they died.

Fire—

The earth aches from man.
At the foot of the line, thirty centimetres of earth.
Another row of the dead.

Fire—

Bones, ashes.
Everyone knows why they died.
Numbers. Names.
Dust. Smoke.

Fire—

In this madness, what is he screaming, wailing
More unruly than the plague, may your string resonate
I love you so much more than ever before
every moment I think of you a hundred times more

Fire—

He prophecies to God what God himself doesn't even know.

4

The photographer stands in front of him for only a few seconds:
he looks; he feels the shadow upon his skin.
A cloud must be covering the sun, he thinks.

He doesn't believe anything.

There is no sun, no cloud.
Isn't.
Only this off-key falsetto song, his own voice,
nothing, but nothing else.

The lock rattles shut upon us.

Translated by Ottilie Mulzet

MY SON'S FIRST PHOTOGRAPH

In Unter den Linden, the even light's aslant.
My little boy and I are in the street,
He seeing, feeling, sniffing and touching the skin
Of the city whose bones I've come to meet.

The dead live here. They're simply everywhere.
Their monuments pulse through the Berlin air,
Beating at the pavement in a dream.
The great wall's shadow falls across the ground
And you can cross it as you would a stream.

A four-year-old can't take in all of that.
The blank gaze is too natural to him.
For him no corpses: war's lost episode
is dots of light along an endless road.

Can I, he asks? I bend down to his height.
It's his first venture in photography.
And, click, we two become a single blur,
A headless apparition, dark on light.

Mother and child: memorialised as one.
The past is past, there's nothing to be done,
Its shadow, an intangible domain:
Elusive yet acute its phantom pain.

Translated by George Szirtes

WINTER DIARY (SELECTIONS)

ACROSS THE RAILS

Just now, there are no directions.
Wind blows and battles from both sides at once,
and—a candle—I gutter. I stand very still

and on both sides the passing walls tremble
and this narrow space buffets and booms,
and the ground bloats and billows under my feet,
and the trams are a threat. It is clear from the creak
they are much too close, parallel on both sides.
They lean in on the turn
and their bulks seem almost to touch.

I am sickened and silly, and everything spins,
the sky, the road under my feet—
two strips of light gush in front and behind
and time curves in with its doubled dark—
something empty circling inside me,
as I stand in this rumbling no-man's land,
these two moving walls squeezing out where I stand.
Fifty seconds, damned to this hell!

A moment, and everything will jerk back:
there will be up and down and out and in,
instead of this vortex: this darkening spin.
The wheels cry out like cats.

STATUES, PARK

A bronze horse beneath empty trees,
the underground's descending stairs—
and underneath the park's blank sky
the vent shafts clatter, roar and sigh.

The summer-gold bath lost in haze.
By crippled shrubs see pool steam rise,
make mist statues: they dissolve, breathe.
Ink-feathered crows peck rotten leaves,

only until the short walk lasts . . .

AROUND THE TREE

In the ice-storm these cats now mate,
light frozen on their soft, black skins.
They stage their hot, furred winter show,
wild things.

The silvered-glass tree snaps and cracks.
I listen, until sleep defeats
these sounds, that sound like prayers and cries,
pained meat.

Just this. Again. From frost and dark
begins the kitten. Life persists.
This brutish sex obliterates,
exists.

THE SUNLIGHT BAR

An indigo curtain. Outside coffee-coloured reeds—
their brush-tips loosened to bend one way,
like flags—and the willow boughs quiver.
Agárd is washed with warm wind.

Only until the train arrives . . .

Until then he is dozing in my arms,
perspiration steaming from his hair,
that innocent scent. He hugs me.
Tiny beads bubble on his nose.

The compartment is bathed in midday light.
Travellers sleep deeply, under some spell.
The tired girl loosens her mouth a little.
The sun winks on her teeth.

Napsugár Pub. For a moment I catch
the name on the saffron board on the shore,
and the sun pours indeed—I sip it gladly.
It reflects off the mirror; strikes my face.

I close my eyes. How he binds
and supports me! Like love, I guess.

ON THE STAIRS

No one tumbled to the courtyard
from the outside corridor—
we descended down the back stairs,
spiralling from the fifth floor,

and my dear friend went before me—
for two hours now thirty-two—
down into the hellish darkness,
into things that lovers do.

We said all the things we could say,
but emotions are not sane,
We made no sense of that devilish
thing that stirs—her, him and pain,

and the pain remains unsolved still,
but we moved onto small talk.
Neither love, nor faith could help us.
We descended as we walked.

Now I leave. She'll mop dark water
her washing machine won't hold:
spins and slops. I'm in the cab now.

It's cold.

TO BE A PLANT

Plump hibiscus. The sun pours only for her!
She feels the windowsill is blood warm.
Her time and being is different from mine.
She tends towards light. Fattens her buds.

Above her a purslain dangles—places
where the blooms died turned to balls of cotton—
and the big poinsettia, leaves faking as flowers.
In the centres its real, lemon blossoms huddle.
Nectar jewels wobble in flawless globes.

Outside snow. Inside jungle.
I stand at the window in the silence, the shaft of sun,
this moment of happiness that leads me nowhere.

Just breathe.
Everything exists, but I need nothing.
I'm alive with my eyes closed,
as the hibiscus:

only until I am called from here . . .

Translated by George Szirtes

THIS DAY

'Wherever I lie is your bed'

1

Imagine this. It was early afternoon
and I was out looking for a new apartment
wondering as I went, what next to do,
while staring vacantly at January stores
their worn-out goods, their seasonal display
and thought of many things along the way—

suddenly everything vanished:
the tram clattered between the houses, over
the bridge, and instead of broad
vistas of river and road
dense fog hung over invisible water—
I stood astonished.

Fog everywhere: anxiety was a tight
cold sleepless night;
that's my life I thought and felt it glide
swiftly away but I wasn't part of the ride;
my life went on without me inside.
I felt it all but saw nothing anywhere
of the rails I was speeding on
safe across the bridge, on water, ground or air,
in the clouds or a plane high above land

with all assurance of reality gone
but for the cold metal barrier in my hand.

Nothing new then for two long minutes, no less.
And anything might happen now I guess.

2

How my tears flowed! I couldn't tell why they flowed
I simply lay beneath you, bearing my load
of happiness. Another apartment. Another town, then
nothing after it, nothing ever again.

I lost that but found you. I lost no more
than what remains. It wasn't heaven's door
that opened but my body. So we meet.
You come and we make our way along the street.

3

I sweep up the waste cuttings of your hair.
Sixteen years together, everywhere.
Squares and apartments. I note a few grey strands.
My life lies there.

Into the pan with them. Are they for disposal?
I'd sooner collect them all, however fine.
Yes, yes I know, I don't throw things away.
But, well, they're mine.

Some pine needles among them. In summer
light sunflower petals. How things drift and fall.
The earth continues spinning. Does it matter?
No, not at all.

4

Who cares what happens: your neck and shoulder alone
interest me as we cross the bridge in the snow
clutching each other. I will expect you home.
Only tramps take their houses with them wherever they go.

I don't care where we are as long as we are together.
A bare floor, a few chairs and a single table.
There's only one thing I desire, no other,
but that one thing is indispensable.

5

Imagine this. I feel I am growing older.
Our home is a fortress: that's the way I am,
Though the edifice is founded on no rock.
Instead we're travelling in each other's warmth
Across the fogbound bridge inside the tram.

And anything might happen, I suppose,
the way it did that first night there, back then.
Though there are only rails and fog. Who knows.
Wherever you go now, come with me again.

Translated by George Szirtes

MARY SPEAKS

We look at each other, child and mother.

Only babies can watch this way:
curious, intense, hungry,
all-understanding, omniscient,
still terribly innocent—

welcome, my godsend,
dear son, little boy.

What's the world like? I can't tell you:
I just sing, like mothers do,
I hug you, suckle you, start
to lull you to sleep to my heart.

Trust. No need to explain.
Whatever happens happens:
I still know, you already know—
accepting, your eyes close.

Translated by Clare Pollard with Anna T. Szabó

DELIVERY ROOM

I'm pacing the corridor, tears
hitting linoleum. Hormones.
In me, in pain, the child stirs.
a needy fist, the uterus pummels,
squeezes him out.

Thrown by waves of vast force
I try to hold to chairs and tables,
Pain racks me, spins me.
Come on then, I'll let it.

*

Animals give birth in dens, but women
must suffer together. In the delivery room,
in the extended, polyphonic wailing,
through narrow darkness, infants
move in mortal fear.

*

This torment is a demon looking for a host:
it catches you, possesses you, becomes you,
here it is: pulsing, edgeless—
two minutes and it ends

and then again, like ocean, hurricane,
its barbaric language
spills from your mouth, primal howl,
inhuman grief.

You cry for him and his seed
thrust into life through your torture
to feed those grasping demons
already here
waiting at this gate.

*

Come out, little naked snail,
your house is alarmed, in danger,
red flame-tongues spill out of its door.
Come out, slippery snail!

*

You weight, hot iron, stone child,
come on, get out! I beg you!
You destroy me I'm destroying you,
get out, my faceless child!

*

Heave. Wrench. Dilate. You cannot do.
For seven hours you tear. Breathe too.

Pray? Swear? Your voice has gone.
It's too much. Too alien.

*

Don't resist, give yourself up,
this suffering is not you,
but this hour is yours:
this child of yours
has to come out.

*

I was born for this. I waited for it.
This child a gift I carry
in my body's suffering basket.
The machine detects a heart beat
in the anxious interior.
It is pulsating rapidly:
pushing his head, push,
expand this exit.

*

I struggle to breathe.
Breathe my whole body.
Oxygen enters,
blackness pours out.

*

It hurts at first but is tolerable,
then it grows unmanageable . . .
surging, consciousness overbrims,
a master, all-pervading,

the woman is a wolf bitch, yelping,
on the iron bed she's pawing
up to her neck in it,
as if in her last minute,
help she is screaming,
screaming and drowning,
but then the wave of pain recedes,
crashes and collapses,
hurries off, who knows what place.
A few breaths, a pause of grace.

*

It's good I'm not alone.
Others help.
Wipe up my blood,
stroke my hand.

Under dark breakers
I sip for air.
I can't help, not yet.
I hold on but can't push.

My shipwrecked child
clings to the slippery
bloodied raft of my body.
My baby.

*

The pain is not bodily.
Geological. I am carved, tectonic.
Boundless shudder.
Raging elements.

*

He knocks, slips through the door
to this airy, wide world:
a child with his full power
set against destruction;

slides through the eye of the needle,
big head, bony mass.
Once out, there he lies.
They are closed in terror:
his fists, his eyes.

Translated by Clare Pollard with Anna T. Szabó

AU LECTEUR

You,
reader,
washing in words,
to soothe yourself or save time
you clean with this used water.
avoiding the oceanic,
soaking in the tolerably tight space.
Aren't you tense?

What do you hope?
For refreshment?
To be rinsed?

Is it enough if it's comfortably
warm?

You stretch out,
fill it completely.

If the poem is a bath, you step out
naked.

Translated by Clare Pollard with Anna T. Szabó

NOT WATER, NOT WIND

Here I die with bare feet.
Thistle. Bone. Barren stone.
I'm a dried-up snail shell.
It's been thirty days. No rain.

Rubble. A broken jar.
I die with bare feet.
I'd die here. I'd die for you.
I'm your servant your servant.

The way. Just go. Walk upwards.
See the Heaven's veil
crack into light. Towards light.
And they stand still.

Angels like locusts.
Glazed fish eyes.
Someone's watching. Someone's watching.
A throne shines.

Wings. Scales. Pelt.
Hooves, locust claws.
A mute mouth gaping,
a woman's breasts. No more!

Don't let me, Lord. Don't let me!
A mutant snail walking.
A baby sliced in two.
A bright sword falling.

The sea's edge is a sword.
Rocks. Teeth. A wheel rotates.

Don't cover your face!
Naked angels twist.

Leave, Evil! Leave!
Red wine on the stone.
Apples spill towards me, fresh fleshed.
I die with bare feet.

Lord show your throne!
Your divine glow!
Someone's watching. Someone's watching.
An eye burns me to bone.

Translated by Clare Pollard with Anna T. Szabó

WOMAN ON A PLAID BLANKET

An afternoon, sunlit,
a terrace, I dozed.
He aimed and he shot.
I kept my eyes closed.

A face calm and strict,
light fills the forehead.
A dream's shadow stuck
at the mouth's edge.

Evening, he's gone—turn
the polaroid picture:
So that's what I am
when I'm not here.

Translated by Clare Pollard with Anna T. Szabó

PERSEPHONE

Just never here, no more no more,
that's all I ever want:
to be not here and something else
another world to haunt.

This underworld should let me go,
I'm anybody's rag.
Always obey, whoever says,
always spread my legs.

I've done this work for forty years,
there is no like, just need,
and two old, needy parents,
who love me but are tired.

Good Mamika still cooks meals
for Papa and for me.
The sweat still wets her forehead,
glasses mist so she can't see.

Mamika, do you cry for me?
I will take care of you
I'll have my home and you will have
your own apartment too.

If Papa didn't drink so hard,
We'd have a separate house
not this dim, tiny kitchen,
this anxious place.

You always begged me, Mami:
to go out in the sun,
I'm wan, my powers weaken . . .
I don't want to be seen.

They want this body anyway.
It isn't hard to get.
Just one quick fuck and we can buy
Papa's cigarette.

This one's up for twenty minutes.
In the kitchen there's a stool
Papa sits on while you prepare
a simple spaetzle meal.

And so we would still live today,
if he didn't come—
that underworldly lover,
that dreaded one.

You waited outside as he pushed
me down and slit my throat . . .
This is the last sacrifice,
my destiny played out.

The killer left the room and you
exchanged politenesses.
Ten minutes later you came in.
Don't recall that bloodied mess!

Good Mami, don't remember . . .
I'm in a different world
if you want to hear my voice
just talk to your girl.

This underworld voice sings now
the cut larynx is healed,
from underground, finally,
the victim's voice is heard.

Hear my voice, Mamika,
tell the other girls:
Marika's done with caring,
she got her other world.

I sacrificed my flesh for you,
and then I gave my blood.
I hope Hades is gentler,
I'm hoping that he's good.

Translated by Clare Pollard with Anna T. Szabó

PROTOCOL

She was a doctor, she would have understood.
She knew all the instruments
and artificial words, sterile rubber gloves,
the smell of disinfection,
the scales on which powders are measured
with such precision, the cold white cloak
in which specialists of the body pass
uniformed like angels,
knew the cool, sure terms of the dead language,
the frozen empathy and objectivity
when it comes to cutting.

They wrote about the texture of her lungs,
the colour of her liver. Accurate,
in exact sentences, those good pathologists.
Now I can see inside the body,
the body she obsessively hid from me
when I was three
and accidentally stepped into her room,
and which, much later, weakly, sick,
she offered me one afternoon
so I could help her get into the bath.
She was not carefully calculating like love.
It was more objective, like trust.

She was beautiful and eighty. Me,
Preparing for my wedding, twenty-three,
relaxed in my flexible body.
She didn't care any more about the long
surgical scar, the deep ditches of her flesh,
the skeleton showing under skin,
the small hips that gave birth to my father
after two days of hard labour.

I didn't examine her, I wasn't staring, but I saw
and she was the same, not other.
I held her almost floating in bathwater.
I never wanted to let go.

Eight years after her death,
looking for another document,
I find the report in a folder.
Just like the chest bone snaps before
the belly is sliced through. Just as,
after separating the internal organs,
the scalpel touches table with a clang.

An alien hand in a rubber glove
grabs my heart and throws it on the scales.

Translated by Clare Pollard with Anna T. Szabó

ACKNOWLEDGEMENTS

This anthology could never have come about without the generosity of so many. First and foremost, the poets themselves, and their invaluable contributions made to Hungarian letters over the past eighty years; the translators of this volume—Anna Bentley, Erika Mihálycsa, Clare Pollard, Ivan Sanders and George Szirtes—whose diligent and brilliant work it has been an honour to include; and the Translators' House located in Balatonfüred, Hungary, under the selfless direction of poet and translator Péter Rácz, where I began working on this anthology in 2018. I also gratefully thank the rightsholders—Veronika Margit Kerek for Ágnes Nemes Nagy, Judit Faludy for Zsuzsa Beney, Tamás Hervay for Gizelly Hervay, Gábor Mezei for Magda Székely—for kindly granting permission to publish the English translations of their work. Gabriel Sanders kindly allowed me to reprint his father's translation of Zsuzsa Takács's 'Dedication', for which I owe him thanks. Anikó Daróczi, Dóra Szekerés, Gábor Schein and Győző Ferencz were instrumental in helping me connect to the rights holders for Zsuzsa Beney, Ágnes Nemes Nagy and Magda Székely, for which I am deeply grateful. Thanks are due as well to Ildikó Koós at the Artisjus Agency for her prompt and kind assistance.

Arc Publications generously allowed translations of poems by Anna T. Szabó to be reprinted from *Trust* (Clare Pollard with Anna T. Szabó trans. 2021). Similarly, Bloodaxe Books has generously allowed translations to be reprinted from *Ágnes Nemes Nagy: The Night of Akhenaton: Selected Poems* (George Szirtes trans., 2004) as well as from the volume of Krisztina Tóth's poetry, *My Secret Life: Selected Poems* (George Szirtes trans., 2025). I extend my warm thanks to both publishers.

Last but not least I would like to thank everyone at Seagull Books, for their tireless advocacy of and support for literature in translation, and especially the visionary Naveen Kishore; Bishan Samaddar and Dwaipayan Mitra for their sensitive editing work; and Sunandini Banerjee for her extraordinary artistry and design.

This volume is dedicated to the memory of Dr Evžen (Jenci) Gál (1957–2024), a beloved and seminal figure for so many in the Czech and Hungarian translation and literature communities, and whose presence is very deeply missed. His extraordinary contribution to my own understanding of Hungarian literature and mentorship and friendship over the years cannot be easily summarized, but hopefully this anthology is one small step in repaying the debt I owe him.

NOTES ON TRANSLATORS

British by birth, **Anna Bentley** has made Budapest her home since 2000. She began to translate Hungarian literature in 2015. Her translations include: the children's classic, Ervin Lazar's *Arnica, the Duck Princess* (Pushkin Children's Press, 2019), Anna Menyhert's *Women's Literary Tradition and Twentieth-Century Hungarian Writers* (Brill, 2019) and a volume of inclusive fairy tales, Boldizsár M Nagy's *A Fairytale for Everyone* (Harper Collins, 2022). She has published short stories, poetry and novel excerpts by Hungarian authors in online journals, including Asymptote's *Translation Tuesday* blog, *Trafika Europe, World Literature Today* and *Hungarian Literature Online*.

Erika Mihálycsa teaches modernist and contemporary British and Irish literature at Babeș-Bolyai University, Cluj-Napoca. A Joyce and Beckett scholar, author of the volume *"A wretchedness to defend": Reading Beckett's Letters* (University of Debrecen Press, 2022) and co-editor of *Retranslating Joyce for the 21st Century* (Brill, 2020), she edited Rareș Moldovan's new, annotated Romanian translation of *Ulysses* (Polirom, 2023). She has translated into Hungarian fiction by Beckett, Flann O'Brien and Patrick McCabe, and into English the experimental fiction of Miklós Szentkuthy and Zsuzsa Selyem.

Ottilie Mulzet has translated over 18 volumes of Hungarian poetry and prose from contemporary authors such as László Krasznahorkai, Szilárd Borbély, Gábor Schein, György Dragomán, László Földényi, István Vörös, Edina Szvoren, Krisztina Tóth and others. Her translation of László Krasznahorkai's *Baron Wenckheim's Homecoming* (New Directions, 2019) was awarded the National Book Award in Translated Literature in 2019, and her translation of Krasznahorkai's *Herscht 07769* was shortlisted for the Gregg Barrios Book in Translation Prize.

Clare Pollard has published five collections of poetry, most recently *Incarnation* (Bloodaxe Books, 2017). Her play *The Weather* (Faber and Faber, 2004) was performed at The Royal Court Theatre. Her translations include *Ovid's Heroines* (Bloodaxe Books, 2013) which she toured as a one-woman show. She has also written a non-fiction title, *Fierce Bad Rabbits: The Tales Behind Children's Picture Books* (Fig Tree. 2019), her first children's novel, *The Untameables* (The Emma Press, 2024), and two adult novels, *Delphi* (Fig Tree, 2022) and *The Modern Fairies* (Penguin 2024).

Ivan Sanders was born in Budapest and subsequently emigrated with his family to the United States in the 1950s. Professor Emeritus at Suffolk College, SUNY, he was also Adjunct Professor at the East. Central European Centre at Columbia University, where he taught Central European cultural history, literature, and Hungarian literature for many years. He was not only a prize-winning translator of such authors as Péter Nádas, Péter Esterházy, Miklós Mészöly, Ádám Bodor, George Konrád and others, but a prolific and renowned essayist on Hungarian and Jewish literary topics.

George Szirtes was born in Budapest but came to the UK as a refugee in the 1950s. He was brought up in London, and went on to study fine art in London and Leeds. His first poetry collection, *The Slant Door* (Martin Secker & Warburg Ltd, 1979), was awarded the Geoffrey Faber Memorial Prize in 1979; his volume *Reel* (Bloodaxe Books, 2004) was awarded the 2004 T. S. Eliot Prize. His memoir of his mother *The Photographer at Sixteen* (MacLehose Press, 2019) was awarded the East Anglian Book Prize for Memoir and Biography as well as the 2020 James Tait Black Memorial Prize for Biography. In addition to over 20 volumes of poetry, Szirtes has also published translations of the work of László Krasznahorkai, Sándor Márai and Magda Szabó. His translation of László Krasznahorkai's *Satantango* (New Directions, 2013) won the 2013 Best Translated Book Award. He is a Fellow of the Royal Society of Literature.

PERMISSIONS
&
PREVIOUS PUBLICATIONS

Ágnes Nemes Nagy

'Trees' (*Fák*), 'Female Landscape' (*A Női taj*), selections from 'Journal' (*Napló*): 'Mind' (*Ész*), 'Nightmare' (*Liderc*), 'Revenge' (*Bosszú*), '*Sic Itur ad Astra*' (*Sic Itur ad Astra*), 'July 1' (*Július 1*), 'You sit and read' (*Ülsz és olvasol*), 'Before the mirror' (*Tükör előtt*), 'Contemplative' (*Elmélkedő*), 'Sincerity' (*Őszinteség*), 'Between' (*Között*), 'Statues' (*Szobrok*), 'Statues I carried' (*Szobrokat vittem*), 'Lazarus' (*Lázár*), 'Revenant' (*A visszajáró*), 'To a Sleeping Figure' (*Az alvóhoz*), 'From the Notebooks of Akhenaton' (*Ekhnáton jegyzeteiből*), 'The Night of Akhenaton' (*Ekhnáton éjszakája*), 'Akhenaton in Heaven' (*Ekhnáton az égben*), 'The Objects' (*A tárgyak*), 'Above the Object' (*A tárgy fölött*), 'Night Oak' (*Éjszákai tölgyfa*), 'Four Pains of Glass' (*Négy kocka,*) 'Spectacle' (*A látvány*), 'The Transformation of a Railway Station' (*Egy pályaudvar átalakítása*), 'When she looked back' (*Hogy visszanézet* [*A távozó*]). In: Ágnes Nemes Nagy, *Összegyűjtött versei* (Budapest: Osiris Kiadó, 1999).

Hungarian originals by kind permission of Veronika Margit Kerek; English translations by kind permission of George Szirtes and Bloodaxe Books. In: Ágnes Nemes Nagy, *The Night of Akhenaton: Selected Poems* (George Szirtes trans.) (Northumberland: Bloodaxe, 2004).

Zsuzsa Beney

'Farewell' (*Búcsú*), 'Lake' (*A tó*), selections from 'Orpheus and Eurydice' (*Orpheus és Eurydiké* [1989]), 'Fugue' (*Fúga*), 'Tattered Details I' (*Elrongyolt részletek I*), 'Tattered Details II' (*Elrongyolt részletek II*), 'Tattered Details III' (*Elrongyolt részletek III*), selections from 'Orpheus and Eurydice' (*Orpheus és Eurydiké* [2003]), 'The River' (*A folyó*), 'Dust' (*Por*), 'I Stand . . .' (*Állok . . .*), 'Into the Spider's Web . . .' (*A pókhálóba . . .*), 'The Guest' (*A vendég*), 'The Tree' (*A fa*), 'Silence' (*Csönd*), 'The Translator' (*A fordító*), 'November, 1956' (*November, 1956*), 'The Mute Word' (*A néma szó*). In: Zsuzsa Beney, *Hulló idő. Összegyűtött versek I. Szerkesztette Dároczi Anikó* (Budapest: Gondolat Kiadó, 2008).

By kind permission of Judith Faludy for the Hungarian originals and George Szirtes for his translations.

Previous publications: 'The River,' 'Dust,' and 'The Translator' (George Szirtes trans.) were first published in *Modern Poetry in Translation*, Series Three, no. 10 (2008).

Ágnes Gergely

'Midnight Burial' (*Éjféli temetés*), 'I Looked into the Well' (*A kútba néztem*), 'Small Town' (*Kisváros*), 'You Are a Sign on my Door Post' (*Ajtófélfámon jel vagy*), 'Bitter Root' (*Keserű gyökerű*), 'Under a Pannonian Sky' (*Pannon ég alatt*), 'Interpretation of Dreams' (*Álomfejtés*), 'Fishes' (*Halak*), 'On the Nature of Light' (*A fény természetéről*), 'Prayer before Lights Out' (*Fohász lámpaoltás előtt*), 'Cemetery in Pannonia' (*Temető Pannóniában*), 'Cosmopolitan' (*Kozmopolita*), 'Shooting in Terézváros' (*Terézvárosi forgatás*), 'Barcarole' (*Barcarola*), 'Charade'

(*Charade*), 'He Comes This Way after Five in the Afternoon' (*Délután öttől erre jár*), 'House at Village's End' (*Faluvégi ház*), 'Pilgrims' (*Zarándokok*). In: Ágnes Gergely, *Úterintő. Összegyűjtött versek* (Budapest: Argumentum, 2006).

'Signal Lights' (*Jelzőlámpák*), 'Church Tower' (*Templomtorony*). In: Ágnes Gergely, *Johanna. Gergely Ágnes versei* (Budapest: Magvető, 1968).

'Psalm 137' (*A 137. zsoltár*), 'From the Years of Barbarism 3' (*A barbárság éveiből 3.*), 'To Miklós Zrínyi' (*Zrínyi Miklóshoz*). In: Ágnes Gergely, *A barbárság éveiből. Huszonöt régebbi és huszonöt újabb vers 1988–1997* (Budapest: A Magyar Írószövetség és a Bélvárosi Könyvkiadó kiadása, 1998).

'Inconnu' (*Inconnu*), 'Inheritance' (*Örökség*). In: Ágnes Gergely, *Viharkabát. Válogatott és új versek* (Budapest: Európa Könyvkiadó, 2016).

All Hungarian originals by kind permission of Ágnes Gergely.

Previous publications: 'Midnight Burial', 'Small Town', 'Barcarole', and 'House at the Village's End' were first published in *Two Lines Journal* Fall 2022.

'I Looked into the Well' and 'Cosmopolitan' were first published on hlo.hu, March 2022.

'Signal Lights,' 'To Miklós Zrínyi', '*Inconnu*', 'Shooting in Terézváros', 'Psalm 137', and 'Interpretation of Dreams' were first published *Europe Now* (The Council for European Studies, New York), June 2019.

Gizella Hervay

'Because our suffocation is sensational' (*Mert fuldoklásunk szenzáció*), 'I'll nail you to my loins' (*Ágyékomra odaszegezlek*), 'I come with fusillade with love' (*Sortűzzel jövök szerelemmel*), 'For you I will kneel' (*Éretted én letérdelek*), 'Loden Coat on the Hook of Eastern Europe' (*Lódenkabát Keleteurópa szegén*), 'I write like one sentenced to death' (*Úgy írok mint a halálraítélt*). In: Gizella Hervay, *Lódenkabát Keleteurópa szegén* (Budapest: Magvető Könyvkiadó, 1983).

'From your womb homeland you expelled me' (*Méhedből kilöktél hazám*). In: Gizella Hervay: *Öt ujjam ötfelé kiált*. Unpublished in poet's lifetime. See: https:/adatbank.ro|iro|htmlk|pdf3078.pdf (accessed 15 November 2025).

'One pain' (*Egyik fájdalom*), 'A beginner at death among you' (*Köztetek kezdő halott*), 'The petrified mother' (*A megkövült anya*), 'Standing alone' (*Szálegyedül*), 'This cell' (*Ez a cella*), 'Blood dries' (*A föld arcára*), 'Grace visits me' (*Meglátogat a kegyelem*). In: Gizella Hervay, *Kettészelt madár. Rekviem* (Budapest: Szépirodalmi Könyvkiadó, 1978).

'Superior pink toilet soap' (*Felsőbbrendű rózsaszín szappan*). Unpublished in poet's lifetime. See: https:/adatbank.ro|iro|htmlk|pdf3078.pdf (accessed 15 November 2025).

'Free Fall. Oratorio for Three Voices' (Excerpt) (*Zuhanások. Oratórium három hangra*). In: Gizella Hervay, *Zuhanások. Oratórium három hangra* (Bucharest: Kriterion Könyvkiadó, 1978).

By kind permission of Tamás Hervay for the Hungarian originals and Erika Mihálycsa for her translations.

Magda Székely

'The Judgement' (*Az ítélet*), 'The Living' (*Az élő*), 'Precipice' (*Szakadék*), 'Shore and Sea' (*Part és tenger*), 'The Damned' (*A kárhozott*), 'Fallen Angel' (*Bukott angyal*), 'Companion' (*Kisérő*), 'Unknown' (*Ismeretlen*), 'Resurrection' (*Feltámadás*), 'Home' (*Otthon*), 'Public Garden' (*Népliget*), 'Rain' (*Eső*), 'Seven Fairy Tales' (*Hét mese*), 'Pelican' (*Pelikán*), 'Thirty' (*Harminc*), 'Madonna' (Madonna), 'January' (*Január*), 'July' (Július), 'An Evening' (*Egy este*), 'The Place' (*A hely*), 'A Drawing' (*Egy rajz*), 'Going Farther' (*A továbbjutás*), 'The Forest' (*Az erdő*), 'Breath' (*Lehelet*), 'Cataract'

(*Hályog*), 'Snow' (*Hó*). In: Magda Székely, *Összes verse* (Budapest: A CET Belvárosi Könyvkiadó kiadása, 2000).

All Hungarian originals by kind permission of Gábor Mezei.

Zsuzsa Takács

'Anima' (*Anima*), 'The Loveliest Movement' (*A legszebb mozdulat*), 'To Leave' (*Kimenni*), 'Continuation (not to ring anyone)' (*Folytatás*), 'Refurbishment' (*Átrendezés*), 'A Hat' (*Egy kalap*), 'The Adoration of the Body' (*A test imádása*), 'Our Master's Absence' (*Gazdánk távolléte*), selection from 'Grammar for Advanced Students' (*Nyelvtan, haladóknak*): 'Dedication' (*Ajánlás*), 'Twelve Experiments' (*Tizenkét kísérlet*), 'Going on' (*Folytatás*), 'Abyss and Hope' (*Mélypont és remény*); selection from 'Premonitions of Mourning' (*A gyász előérzete*): 'I Started Awake' (*Fölriadtam*), 'Machines Do' (*A gépek lélegzenek*), 'For Seventeen Days' (*Tizenhetedik napja*), 'For Twenty-Three Days' (*Huszonharmadik napja*), 'From Now On' (*Mától korán esteledik*), 'If Anybody Touched Me' (*Ha érintene bárki*), 'The Time Comes' (*Egyszer csak*), 'Postscript' (*Utóirat*)]; 'If We Indeed Have Souls' (*Ha van lelkünk ugyan*), 'Accept!' (*Fogadd el! Fogadd el!*), 'With Blind Hope in a Café' (*Egy körúti kávézóban*), 'Blind Hope Weakening' (*A Vak Remény gyöngülése*), 'In September '43' (*Negyvenhárom szeptemberében*). In: Zsuzsa Takács, *A vak remény. Összegyűjtött és új versek* (Budapest: Magvető Kiadó, 2018).

'Dedication: In Memory of My Parents' (*Ajánlás: szüleim emlékének*) In: Zsuzsa Takács, *Jaj a győztesnek!* (Budapest: Vigília Kiadó, 2008).

Hungarian originals by kind permission of Zsuzsa Takács; translations by kind permission of George Szirtes and Erika Mihálycsa.

Previous publications: 'If We Indeed Have Souls' (George Szirtes trans.) was first published in *Continental Magazine*, April 2022.

'Dedication: In Memory of My Parents' (Ivan Sanders trans.), by kind permission of Gabriel Sanders; 'A Hat', 'The Adoration of the Body', and 'Our Master's Absence' (George Szirtes trans.) were first published in *The Hungarian Quarterly* 52, no. 204 (Winter 2011).

Zsófia Balla

'Flowers' (*Virágok*), 'In the Other Wing of the Palace' (*Palota másik szárnyában*), 'Morning prayer' (*Reggeli ima*), 'On the Edges' (*Széleken*), 'Descent to Hell' (*Pokolraszállás*), 'The Rose' (*A rózsa*), 'Sky and Earth' (*Ég és föld*), 'The Third Tale' (*A harmadik történet*), 'The Sign of the Goat' (*A Bak jegye*), 'Afterwards' (*Azután*), 'In Creation' (*A teremtésben*), 'The Object' (*A tárgy*), 'Bare Trees' (*Csupasz fák*), 'A Hundred Years Ago Tomorrow' (*Holnap száz éve*), 'My Grandmother in an Oval Frame' (*Nagyanyám ovális keretben*), 'Old Chorale' (*Régi korál*), Selection from 'The Two Halves of Life (*Fragments for Miklós Gáspár Tamás*)' (*Az élet két fele* [*Töredékek Tamás Gáspár Miklósnak*]): '(The Dream)', (*Az álom*), '(Night in Koloszvár)', (*Kolozsvár éjjel*); A Gloss on the Ten Commandments' (*Glossza a Tízparancsolathoz*), 'Sentimental Research (*Erzelmi kutatások*)', 'Home' (*Haza*). In: Zsófia Balla, *Az élet két fele. Versek 1965–2019* (Budapest: Kalligram, 2019).

Previous publications: 'The Third Tale,' 'The Sign of the Goat,' 'In Creation,' and 'The Object' (George Szirtes trans.) were first published in *The Hungarian Quarterly*, no. 179 (2005).

'Flowers' and 'A Hundred Years Ago Tomorrow' (Anna Bentley trans.) were first published on hlo.hu, 15 August 2018.

'A Gloss on the Ten Commandments' (Anna Bentley trans.) was first published in *Continental Magazine*, December 2022.

By kind permission of Zsófia Balla for the Hungarian originals and George Szirtes and Anna Bentley for their translations.

Zsuzsa Rakovszky

'They Were Burning Dead Leaves' (*Avart égettek*), 'Insomnia' (*Az elalvás nehézségei*), 'From the Dutch School' (A *németalföldi terem*), 'Decline and Fall' (*Decline and Fall*), 'Old Women of My Childhood' (*Gyerekkori öreg nők*), 'Journey Back in Time' (*Visszaút az időben*), 'Phantoms' (*Kísértetek*), 'Triptych' (*Triptichon*), 'Song about Time' (*Dal az időről*), 'Final Days' (*Az utolsó napok*). In: Zsuzsa Rakovszky, *Állapotváltozások. Válogatott veresk 1981–2019* (Budapest: Magvető Kiadó, 2020).

'In an Alpha State' (*Alfa-állapotban*), 'Star' (*Csillag*), 'Autumn' (*Ősz*), 'Forest' (*Erdő*). In: Zsuzsa Rakovszky, *Fortepan. Versek* (Budapest: Magvető Kiadó, 2016).

'Face. Rembrandt, Portrait of Aechje Claedr' (*Arc. Rembrandt: Aechje Claesdr portrétja*), 'Dream. Tivadar Kosztka Csontváry: Roman Bridge at Mostar' (*Álom. Csontváry Kosztka Tivadar: Római híd Mosztarban*), selections from 'Polemic in Living Time' (*Vita élő időben*), 'A.' (*A.*), 'B.' (*B.*), 'A.' (*A.*), 'Gnostic' (*Gnosztikus*). In: Zsuzsa Rakovszky, *Vita elő időben* (Budapest: Magvető, 2023).

By kind permission of Zsuzsa Rakovszky for the Hungarian originals and George Szirtes and Oxford University Press for the translations of 'They Were Burning Dead Leaves', 'Insomnia', 'From the Dutch School', 'Decline and Fall', and 'Old Women of My Childhood'. In: Zsuzsa Rakovszky, *New Life* (George Szirtes trans. and selection) (Oxford and New York: Oxford University Press, 2004).

Krisztina Tóth

'New Year's Eve' (*Szilveszter*), 'Clothes' (*Ruhák*). In: *Porhó. Új és válogatott versek* (Budapest: Magvető, 2001).

'Shadowgrass' (*Árnyékfű*), 'The Mouse' (*Az egérről*), 'Machine Voice' (*Géphang*). In: Krisztina Tóth, *Síró ponyva. Versek 2000–2003* (Budapest: Magvető, 2004).

'East-Europe Triptych' (*Kelet-európai triptichon*). In: Krisztina Tóth, *Magas labda: versek* (Budapest: Magvető, 2009).

'Sleeper' (*Hosszúalvó*), 'Tyrannosaurus Rex' (*Zsarnokgyík*), 'Any Country in the World' (*A világ minden országa*), 'Cold Weather' (*Hideg idő*), 'Time, time, time' (*Idő, idő, idő*), 'Duration' (*Futamidő*). In: Krisztina Tóth: *Világadapter* (Budapest: Magvető, 2016).

'Song of the Secret Life' (*Dal a titkos életről*), 'Vatera' (*Vatera*), 'Where' (*Ahol*). In: Krisztina Tóth, *Balnadal* (Budapest: Magvető, 2021).

'Oven Glove' (*Edényfogó*). In: *Élet és irodalom* 65, nos 51–52 (December 2021).

By kind permission of Krisztina Tóth for the Hungarian originals and George Szirtes for his translations. By kind permission as well of Bloodaxe Books for the Hungarian originals and English translations of 'New Year's Eve', 'Sleeper', 'Tyrannosaurus Rex', 'Any Country in the World', 'Cold Weather', 'Time, time, time', 'Duration', 'Song of the Secret Life', 'Vatera', and 'Where'. In: Krisztina Tóth, *My Secret Life: Selected Poems* (George Szirtes, trans.) (Hexham: Bloodaxe Books, 2025).

Previous publications: 'East-Europe Triptych' and 'The Mouse' (Ottilie Mulzet trans.) were first published on lyrikline.de.

Anna T. Szabó

''44, Tiresias' (*'44. Teiresziasz*), 'My Son's First Photograph' (*Fiam első képére*), selections from 'Winter Diary' (*Téli napló*): 'Across the Rails' (*Átkelés a síneken*), 'Statues, Park' (*Szobrok, liget*), 'Around the Tree' (*A fa körül*), 'The Sunlight Bar' (*Napsugár Pub*), 'On the Stairs' (*A lepscőn*), 'To Be a Plant' (*Növénynek lenni*); 'This Day' (*A mai nap*). In: Anna T. Szabó, *Vagyok. Összegyűjtött ás új versek* (Budapest: Magvető, 2022).

'Mary Speaks' (*Mária mondja*), 'Delivery Room' (*Szülőszoba*), 'Au Lecteur' (*Au Lecteur*), 'Not Water, Not Wind' (*Se víz, se szél*), 'Woman on a Plaid Blanket' (*Fekvő nő kockás pokrócon*), 'Persephone' (*Perszephoné*), 'Protocol'

(*Jegyzőkönyv*). In: Anna T. Szabó, *Trust* (Clare Pollard with Anna T. Szabó trans, Sasha Dugdale introd.) (Tormorden: Arc Publications, 2021).

All Hungarian originals by kind permission of Anna T. Szabó; translations by kind permission of Anna T. Szabó, Clare Pollard and George Szirtes. By kind permission as well of Arc Publications for 'Mary Speaks', 'Delivery Room', 'Au Lecteur', 'Not Water, Not Wind', 'Woman on a Plaid Blanket', 'Persephone', and 'Protocol'. In: Anna T. Szabó, *Trust* (Clare Pollard with Anna T. Szabó trans., Sasha Dugdale introd.) (Tormorden: Arc Publications, 2021).